COUNSELLING AND SOCIAL WORK

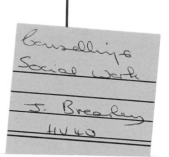

· COUNSELLING IN CONTEXT ·

Series editors
Moira Walker and Michael Jacobs
University of Leicester

Counselling takes place in many different contexts: in voluntary and statutory agencies; in individual private practice or in a consortium; at work, in medical settings, in churches and in different areas of education. While there may be much in common in basic counselling methods (despite theoretical differences), each setting gives rise to particular areas of concern, and often requires specialist knowledge, both of the problems likely to be brought, but also of the context in which the client is being seen. Even common counselling issues vary slightly from situation to situation in the way they are applied and understood.

This series examines twelve such areas, and applies a similar scheme to each, first looking at the history of the development of counselling in that particular context; then at the context itself, and how the counsellor fits into it. Central to each volume are chapters on common issues related to the specific setting and questions that may be peculiar to it but could be of interest and value of counsellors working elsewhere. Each book will provide useful information for anyone considering counselling, or the provision of counselling in a particular context. Relationships with others who work in the same setting whether as counsellors, managers or administrators are also examined; and each book concludes with the author's own critique of counselling as it is currently practised in that context.

Current and forthcoming titles

COUNSELLING AND SOCIAL WORK

Judith Brearley

OPEN UNIVERSITY PRESS
Buckingham · Philadelphia

Open University Press
Celtic Court
22 Ballmoor
Buckingham
MK18 1XW

email: enquiries@openup.co.uk
world wide web: www.openup.co.uk

and
325 Chestnut Street
Philadelphia, PA 19106, USA

First Published 1995
Reprinted 1996, 2000

A catalogue record of this book is available from the British Library

ISBN 0 335 19002 2 (pb)

Library of Congress Cataloging-in-Publication Data
Brearley, Judith, 1941–
Counselling and social work / Judith Brearley.
p.   cm. — (Counselling on context)
Includes bibliographical references and index.
ISBN 0–335–19002–2
1. Social service.   2. Social service — Psychological aspects.
3. Counseling.   I. Title.   II. Series.
HV40.B823   1994
360.3'23—dc20
94–22205   CIP

Typeset by Graphicraft Ltd, Hong Kong
Printed in Great Britain by St Edmundsbury Press Ltd,
Burry St Edmunds, Suffolk

Contents

Dedicated to the memory of Jock Sutherland

Series editors' preface

There is no one profession that can be said to have spawned counselling. Counsellors bring to their work a variety of backgrounds and initial training. Freud certainly hoped that psychoanalysis would develop as a distinct profession that was neither medical nor clerical. Counselling and psychotherapy have to a large measure fulfilled that wish.

Nevertheless some books in this series locate counselling within a definite professional setting. Viewed positively, social work has a rich and varied history; viewed negatively, it has been the perpetual pawn of bureaucratic and policy changes and a convenient scapegoat for society's ills. Its history includes a notable tradition of individual case-work, reminiscent of much counselling and psychotherapeutic thinking and practice. There is a strong link between early case work and psychoanalytic thought. Social workers have often been the sole means of making available to the wider community the benefits of psychological understanding and what we now call counselling skills. While not forgetting the significance of early voluntary agencies, it was primarily social workers who were firmly community based, offering help to those who would not receive it elsewhere.

Social work as a profession attracted many who wished to work therapeutically with individuals, including those who have since moved into counselling as a way of continuing to give individuals time and space without always having to act upon them to make them change. Social work training has always drawn upon the expertise of psychologists and therapists (albeit from time to time of different persuasions, because fashions change in social work training too). Such links with the world of psychotherapy continue now in the social work students who look for placements in counselling services as a part of their practical training.

For such students, for social workers who long to be able to manage better the balance between the different demands on them, and for those who develop and implement social policy, Judith Brearley's book is a fine and thorough review of the tensions within the social work profession, as it seeks to meet the demands of the legislators, of society at large, as well as the preferences of the workers themselves for counselling individuals and families. She makes it clear that social workers have often borne the brunt of society's indignation when the awful state of people's lives (and particularly their children) are revealed in court cases and reports of inquiries. Social workers have to carry both the outspoken demands of politicians and public, as well as (more importantly) the unmet needs of their clients. All this calls for a careful balance between working with individual issues and with the roots of such issues in social structures. If it appears there is little power or room for manoeuvre in either direction, those who work as counsellors and social workers know that the pursuit of one direction alone is not sufficient. Judith Brearley identifies the issues, highlights the pressures, exposes the dilemmas, in a way which is both scholarly and also sensitive.

This series of books generally suggests the need for greater investment of money, time and energy in the caring professions and other allied agencies. This particular volume reminds us of the societal structures which professionals such as social workers seek to address, while always having to accommodate to the weight of societal pressures themselves. It points to the tensions which professionals have in their role as society's agents. It is both supportive to the social work profession and a warning to other professional groups that there is more to every context than case work alone.

Moira Walker
Michael Jacobs

Preface

When I was approached by the Editors to submit a proposal for this book, and as I then struggled with seemingly intractable dilemmas of definition of the subject matter, it did not at first occur to me that a subjective look at elements of my own background might provide a way forward. As someone with thirty years' professional involvement in social work and counselling, I am bound to be personally implicated in the subject; some declaration of my biases and emotional reactions, including sadness and pride, might also help the reader to evaluate what follows.

The decision of a naive seventeen-year-old to study sociology at the London School of Economics gives evidence of early yet substantial interest in the contextual concerns of this book. Already in place was a tentative plan to become a medical social worker, or almoner to use the title then current. Members of my own family were involved in such work. My grandfather was an elected member of the local authority children's committees, and used to take me when still quite a small child on his visits to children's homes; my mother was an unqualified almoner until she gained her professional qualification at the age of sixty-one. I therefore had a degree of familiarity with social work's challenges and rewards, and found myself rejecting other options and steering a relatively single-minded path towards that goal. Medical social work in the early 1960s had a very large component of what would now be labelled counselling values and skills. I recall vividly that there was an elitist aspect to the work; fully qualified workers were in short supply, posts offering excellent supervision and favourable conditions for in-depth work were plentiful, the close association with the medical profession and the caricatured image of being 'proper' or 'nice' lent an aspect of stability and respectability and a feeling of being valued. I also recall how readily I became absorbed in helping individuals and families from all walks of life in their struggle to cope with the adjustments and losses associated with illness. I now realize how narrow was this specialist focus. At that time there was little awareness of how to work with groups, neighbourhoods or communities, of contributing to wider policy making or of challenging unfair discrimination, and the legislative component of the work was almost non-existent. However, it was invaluable in helping me to acquire counselling principles and skills of a high order.

After gaining experience in general practice and paediatrics, in practice teaching of social workers and lecturing to medical and nursing students, I felt that a move to full-time social work education was the next obvious step. This coincided with the burgeoning of new departments of social work following the Kilbrandon and Seebohm Reports, and the consolidation of shared training for all branches of social work rather than the previous separate specialisms. The chance to prepare people for a wider repertoire of roles in an expanding service was to me exciting and positive.

My own professional development at this point, the early 1970s, took two extra and apparently divergent turns. One was to embark on a full training in psychoanalytical psychotherapy, while the other was to engage in consultancy to community groups such as the playgroup movement, and to attempt to influence the policy of residential care of troubled young people. This simultaneous conjunction of concern to understand unconscious inner subjective reality with practical involvement in the politics of social provision never felt contradictory; indeed, these aspects complemented one another and gave me a much more rounded view of people's real needs. All this expresses something about which I feel very strongly – an urge to integrate the inner and outer aspects of life rather than to compartmentalize them.

One interest which for me served to hold together these aspects rather than to polarize them was a fascination with group dynamics, and I made various attempts, both experiential and theoretical, to understand and work with them. Harold Bridger's work was particularly influential; he helped me towards a real grasp of the value of paying at least as much attention to the *ways* in which work groups address their tasks as to the *content* of those tasks. His concern with context, with the need to identify and pay attention to the relevant environment of an enterprise, was an equally significant area of learning for me.

An even greater influence was Dr J.D. (Jock) Sutherland, who returned to Edinburgh on his retirement from the post of Medical Director of the Tavistock Clinic, and with others founded the Scottish Institute of Human Relations in 1970. He was deeply committed to psychoanalytic understanding of the person in the context of their significant relationships, to the advanced training of psychotherapists, and to the ways in which such understanding and training could be made available to those suffering psychological distress of all sorts throughout the community (Sutherland 1971).

These mentors encouraged and enabled me to pursue such concerns by sharing in establishing a two-year human relations and counselling course, by helping to develop the skills of marital counsellors through regular case discussion groups, adequate in-depth training and supportive organizational structures, and by involvement in the training of child psychotherapists.

It can be seen, therefore, that my chief professional concerns – namely, social work practice and education, counselling and psychotherapy, and consultancy to groups and organizations – strongly resonate with the theme of counselling in the specific context of social work.

It is with some sadness and frustration, therefore, that I regard both the recent very serious vicissitudes of the social work profession and also the tensions and territorial disputes at the boundaries of activities labelled 'counselling'. In the middle of the turbulence are all those who from time to time need the services of counsellors or social workers. These potential service users, in becoming clients, bring with them their experiences of an increasingly stressful environment, their needs, relationships and feelings. How they are responded to, in the context of history, societal change and professional dilemmas, is the subject of this book.

Acknowledgements

I have been influenced by far more friends, colleagues, clients, students and consultees than it is possible to mention by name; the learning from them has been immeasurable, and I am grateful for it. I should like to record my particular thanks to Marjorie Noble, my original mentor in medical social work, and to Nita Brown, Mary Hart and Catherine Smithson for keeping me in touch with the real world of current social work. Don Bryant helped me to express myself more clearly, and Dave Brown and Paul Newman gave generous help with computing and word-processing skills. Paul's wife, Alison Newman, sadly died shortly before the completion of this book, but her wisdom and humour sustained my efforts, as did Rosemary Nixon's constant encouragement and emotional support.

· ONE ·

The development of counselling in social work

The aim of this book is to clarify the nature of counselling as it is practised within the specific context of social work. The central concern of the book, as indeed of the whole series, is with *context*, in recognition of the fact that it is impossible to understand any phenomenon in isolation from its environment and the setting in which it finds expression. The context of social work in particular happens to be complex and multifaceted; all the more reason, therefore, why we need to make the effort to tease out the impact of the social work context on the practice of counselling.

Counselling and social work are not two separate entities: they have much in common. Although they share ancient roots, both are relatively recently established as separate fields of study unlike, say, medicine or law. Both are rapidly changing, and seem likely to continue to do so, in response to shifting needs and attitudes in the wider society on the one hand, and to internal heart-searching and rethinking by their practitioners on the other. As a consequence of this, the interface, overlap, relationship and interaction between them is also continuously being renegotiated. Any debate on counselling and social work must acknowledge these basic features. My aim is to avoid any notion of defining social work or counselling as static disciplines, and I have tried to convey the pace of change and the quality of their mutual influence in a dynamic way; this, for me, is a riskier and yet more exciting process.

In the mid-1960s, when the term 'counselling' was beginning to become current in Britain, I recall many social workers arguing that little distinction existed between counselling and social work. 'Isn't that exactly what we are doing most of the time?' they would have said, with some justification. Nowadays I hear social workers saying the reverse: 'Is there any place at all for real counselling in social work? And even if there is, are we properly trained to do it?' Such questioning, and the contradictions it expresses, highlight the need to look at our subject matter in a rigorous way, from different vantage points, and to define it very carefully. First, I want to look more closely at the scope of social work.

WHAT IS SOCIAL WORK?

Social work is not only a relatively young profession but it is also one which derives more directly and more substantially from the particular society of which it is a part than is the case with other professions. Hence its functions and its modes of operation are substantially dependent on existing social structures and are to a great extent affected by the various processes of change within them.

(Butrym 1976: ix)

. . . social work is very much a product of our time, and we will find at best only parallels with other times and other societies. Modern social work can only be understood within the context of modern society.

(Timms 1970: 19)

These statements illustrate the difficulty of giving a short simple definition of social work; it would be like offering a snapshot when a video film is needed. But they do underline the basic tension in any thinking about the nature of social work; the tension between concern for the individual in distress on the one hand and a requirement to work within the bounds – moral, political, legal and economic – of society on the other. Battles have raged over definitions. Social work cannot avoid raising issues that mirror fundamental conflicts in society itself. How far should social work espouse a maintenance function, and to what extent should it offer a radical critique of the *status quo*? What is the right balance between giving a service and sharing in policy formulation? How broad or narrow should be its remit, and who decides where to draw the line? Although I recall questions like this being asked in the 1960s, the emphasis was much more on what was then called social casework.

Social casework

At one time the term 'casework' was central in social work practice and education, but it now has a dated connotation, and has been little used since the mid-1970s. It described the very large segment of social work practice concerned primarily with individuals and families, as opposed to work with groups or communities. The origins of social casework go back to the Victorian era, reflecting the individualist culture of that time. It has developed considerably over the years, and from it since the 1950s has emerged a whole conceptual framework for intervention with individuals and families. Even though the terminology has now changed, many of the values behind the original thinking, although adapted to suit radically changing circumstances, remain current. In social casework, great emphasis has always been placed on the *relationship* between helper and helped. This relationship, which as we shall see is at the core of all counselling, has been a persistent theme in the historical development of counselling in social work.

Social casework was usually seen as one of the helping processes within social work, differentiated from other modes of help such as group work, community work and residential work by its focus on the single instance, the case. Perlman (1973) points out that it has been the most theoretically developed, the most generally and widely used and the most readily taught process. However, it is *not* a universal panacea; it cannot *tackle* social problems, whether poverty, unemployment or delinquency, but works *with* the person or family affected by these factors. Its theoretical emphasis and methodology does not equip its practitioners adequately to assess or treat social problems.

> Case by case we may help this or that person pull up out of a social quagmire or to find some more tolerable breathing space within it. But the causes of that quagmire and the effects of its presence will not be eradicated by the case method, and we must not pretend to this.
>
> (Perlman 1973: 8)

This awareness of the limitations of social casework can help us to understand the serious difficulties facing social work today. At one extreme there is the danger of unrealistic claims being made for an approach which has its own constraints; at the other is the risk of labelling such a case method as useless. Perlman makes a spirited case for a two-pronged approach – the retention of casework because of the worth of the individual and the inhumanity of not offering some help while waiting for social reform, coupled with attempts to bring about social change, not only by the politicians and activists but also by all those who, as staff of various agencies, members of professions, or as informed concerned citizens, are struggling against injustice. Much of what Perlman says about social casework is equally applicable to counselling, and such considerations may prove helpful in the attempt to elucidate the murky common ground and appropriate differentiation between counselling and social work.

COUNSELLING

By contrast with 'social casework', the term 'counselling' was scarcely used by social workers until the mid-1960s. In other fields of work it had a longer pedigree; there had been marriage guidance counsellors since the 1940s, and by 1951 Carl Rogers was able to draw on a substantial body of American literature and practice from the previous ten years. In Britain it was not until the publication of Paul Halmos's *The Faith of the Counsellors* in 1965 that the role of counselling began to be made explicit and that practice began to develop in a substantial way. This was a thought-provoking, controversial and scholarly critique which led to much more discussion and debate about the nature of counselling than had previously existed. Halmos held up a mirror to the implicit beliefs about helpgiving prevalent at that time, and to some extent still held. He saw such beliefs as very powerful, extremely contradictory or paradoxical, even irreconcilable. It is worth reiterating some of them here, as they help to set the scene for evaluation of what has happened since:

- The conviction that intervention is much more effective when it involves spontaneous warmth and affection, and equally that it requires carefully thought-out technique.
- A simultaneous belief in both the rationality and the irrationality of clients, and related to this, the contradictory need for both personal involvement and objectivity on the part of the counsellor.
- A commitment to non-directiveness when this is in fact impossible to achieve, and even in some respects undesirable.
- A paradoxical use of didactic training methods, even though it is clear that the required insight is not imparted through such methods.
- A sense of both the interminability of the helping process and the need to achieve closure or to show that real change has been achieved.

Halmos's ideas provide the clearest starting point for tracing the historical development of counselling:

This century has seen the development of a new professional activity practised by people of widely varying training and expertise. Psychiatrists, lay and medical psychotherapists, clinical psychologists, social caseworkers of several kinds, and some others, have all learned to share the assumptions and values of the new philanthropic expertise of helping through caring–listening–prompting . . . I call the practitioners of this expertise 'counsellors' . . . Basically and essentially all practitioners of counselling . . . have a common origin and a common aim: their common ancestor is the giver of spiritual solace and their common aim is health, sanity, a state of unspecified virtue, even a state of grace, or merely a return to the virtues of the community, adjustment . . . Above all, all counselling procedures share a method: they are all 'talking cures', semantic exercises, they all attempt treatment through clarification of subjective experiences and meanings.

(Halmos 1965: 2)

Halmos continues to discuss the dilemma absolutely central to the current debate, which is about how the term 'counselling' should be used. Having identified considerable common ground among a wide range of practitioners, he deliberately chooses to use the term in a very comprehensive way, grouping together a whole range of procedures. He includes psychotherapy and social casework, and does not rule out an advice-giving, interventionist or directive component, which he believes existed even if not always acknowledged. In justifying this broad usage, he asserts that the highest common factor in all these activities is at least *important and characteristic enough* to justify their inclusion under the one concept. He even goes further to suggest that this common factor is not only large but is the *decisive part* of the various helping procedures; a more radical view with which he expects some people to disagree.

The radical view is echoed closely in the definition made twenty years later by the British Association for Counselling (BAC):

People become engaged in counselling when a person, occupying regularly or temporarily the role of counsellor, offers or agrees explicitly to offer time, attention and respect to another person or persons temporarily in the role of client.

(BAC 1985: 1)

The BAC's emphasis on explicit offering or agreeing is deliberate, as it is seen as 'the dividing line between the counselling task and *ad hoc* counselling and is the major safe-guard of the rights of the consumer.' (BAC 1985: 2) This distinction is very difficult to maintain when counsellor and client occupy more than one role in relation to each other, as in much modern social work practice. Then 'the tidiness of a theoretical definition may not be easy to replicate in the complex and often messy and confusing empirical world in which we all have to live' (Woolfe *et al.* 1989: 5). This is for me an important consideration in attempting to assess the place of counselling in present-day social work.

ANCIENT ROOTS? SOME DEVELOPMENTAL THEMES

We need to beware of too facile and indiscriminate attempts to trace the historical development of either social work or counselling. It is extremely difficult to obtain an accurate picture of past practice on which we all too readily impose our own value judgements:

> The failure to set the ideas of a particular period within the context of their time does not apply only to attempts to understand the immediate past of social work. It is often assumed that contemporary social work has a direct connection with earlier and well-established traditions of help . . . What is this tradition and how is social work articulated with it?
>
> (Timms 1970: 13)

What follows, therefore, is a cautious sampling of strands from both the distant and more recent past which may throw light on current practice issues. The focus at this preliminary stage will be on helpgiving in general, rather than prematurely attempting to discriminate between counselling and social work.

First, I want to look at the issue of motivation. Undoubtedly, religious motives formed a significant underpinning of social work as well as many other forms of voluntary helping efforts. Judaism, Christianity, Islam and other great world religions have always laid on their followers the obligation to give personal service – to feed the hungry, heal the sick, comfort the weak – as well as to give alms. The advantage to the recipient was not the only concern; the salvation of the soul of the giver was also a significant factor. Other motivating factors throughout history include guilt on the part of the more fortunate, the wish to exert power, fear lest the poor might threaten the livelihood of the rich and the fabric of society, and even genuine sympathy for the underdog. The link between help-giving and motivation, whether religious or philosophical, highlighted questions and moral judgements about the causation of distress and inadequacy, and hence about appropriate responses. Exploration of the mixed motives underlying modern forms of personal help-giving, and the changing views about the aetiology of personal difficulty, is a persistent theme throughout this book. Second, I find it helpful to identify historically some crucial elements of the helping process. The Old Testament provides useful examples. Then the equivalent of counsellors were men of state, giving advice, guidance and direction in the context of the royal court, with the king deciding which course to follow. But there are also examples of individuals finding counsel through someone close to them – a friend or mother. Exodus 18 contains a remarkable account of the modern-day equivalent of work consultancy or supervision: Moses' father-in-law, Jethro, comes upon Moses exhausting himself helping people with their problems, and strongly advocates careful discrimination of tasks and judicious delegation as better ways of coping. The Psalms (16: 7, 73: 24) and Isaiah (9: 6, 28: 29) speak of God giving counsel. The New Testament takes this idea further by adding to the previous use of 'counsel' – consulting together on a course of action – the extra concepts of being alongside as helper, advocate, comforter, and speaks of the Holy Spirit in these terms. Through the ages, help and support in distress or perplexity has been given spontaneously through the medium of listening attentively, in an accepting uncritical way.

Developments in the nineteenth century

The centrality of personal relationships in modern social work and counselling parallels the charitable work of educated middle-class ladies in Victorian times. Although sometimes caricatured, the leading figures – for example, Elizabeth Fry, Josephine Butler and Octavia Hill – achieved great reforms by using a wide repertoire of approaches evident in modern social work. One conviction they shared was the necessity of underpinning their practical help with sensitive personal contact. For example, Octavia Hill, a Christian Socialist, stressed the importance of friendship for successful housing management, and gave a paper on the 'Importance of Aiding the Poor without Almsgiving', while Elizabeth Fry, a devout Quaker, went alone to visit women prisoners living in utmost depravity, as a mother with other mothers, reassuring them and helping them to learn and to be productive. 'Being alongside' as well as 'doing for', in an unassuming, self-giving, committed and non-patronizing manner, and thereby demonstrating and giving expression to their own religious beliefs, were hallmarks of the Victorians' approach.

The role of the State remained minimal until well into the nineteenth century. Instead there was a range of charitable and reforming efforts evident in many social institutions, including schools, hospitals, prisons and orphanages. Additionally, charitable societies provided financial or practical help to those in danger of becoming destitute. The system was one of 'haphazard charity and philanthropy'.

(Young and Ashton 1956: 7)

The first half of the nineteenth century was a time of massive social change, devastating in its scale and pace. The doubling of the population coupled with the Industrial Revolution resulted in large masses of people living in abject poverty, in appalling housing conditions, having little or no education, and suffering inhumane working conditions. The gulf between rich and poor widened; the rich seemed indifferent to the circumstances and needs of the poor, and an atmosphere of mutual hostility characterized their relationships. Not surprisingly, ill-health, vagrancy and crime, especially in the cities and industrial centres, became desperately serious. The initial response was a striking increase in the number of charities and philanthropic associations, reflecting a firmly held belief in the value of this approach as opposed to either drastic reform of the social structure or greater intervention by the state. Unfortunately, the very diversity and number of charities, the piecemeal way in which they had come into being, and their idiosyncratic, indiscriminate modes of giving help, meant that many needy people were bypassed while a minority exploited the system. As C.S. Loch complained in 1882:

These charities . . . stand one by one, isolated like lighthouses; but unfortunately not, like lighthouses, placed with care precisely on those points of the dangerous coastline of pauperism, where their lights will save from shipwreck the greatest number of distressed passers-by.

(quoted by Woodroofe 1962: 23)

Even education was largely left to denominational schools paid for by private subscription, to Sunday Schools and to the Mechanics' Institutes, until the 1870 Education Act provided a system of basic public education to supplement such voluntary effort. Likewise, in industrial welfare, the efforts of Robert Owen, a Quaker whose vision of ways of improving the conditions of working-class life through provision of housing, education and health care was clearly demonstrated in his New Lanark mills and village, were ignored. State intervention was piecemeal and hesitant. In 1833 and 1847, legislation limited the working hours, first of children and then of women and youths, and appointed factory inspectors. Lord Shaftesbury's efforts led to the Mines Acts of 1842 and 1850, but it was not until 1875 that the notorious problem of little boy chimney sweeps was effectively curbed by legislation. These measures demonstrate that sympathy for children was gradually increasing, but equally it illustrates that neglect and abuse of children was prevalent and persistent.

Other major and interrelated developments of the nineteenth century were the enactment and working of the 'New Poor Law', and the establishment of the Charity Organization Society in 1869. These greatly influenced the climate of opinion in which social work as we know it today began to emerge.

A Royal Commission on the Poor Law had reported in 1834. The resulting new legislation aimed to force the able-bodied to seek relief in the workhouse or not at all, and to deter all but the most needy from seeking any relief. Its intentionally harsh and stigmatizing approach created as many problems as it solved, through inadequate and demoralizing 'outdoor' relief (i.e. in the home), the unmanageable burden imposed on relatives, and the family break-up it created. The demeaning conditions of the workhouse caused untold misery to the poor for the next 50 years. Perhaps these very strict and punitive measures paved the way for a more humanitarian approach by the 1890s. Shifts in public opinion increased sympathy towards the old and chronically sick, and long-held assumptions that the poor were entirely responsible for their own fate began to be questioned.

Equally influential was the growth of the Charity Organization Society (COS). C.S. Loch, its founder, wanted to channel his energy and idealism by creating something which would be based on clearly articulated principles and which would introduce some order into the chaos which then existed. He shared with most others of his day the basic assumption that if people were not 'self-dependent' it was generally because of some failing of character rather than the impact of social conditions. This notion led the COS into a preoccupation with trying, often unsuccessfully, to separate out the 'deserving' poor from the 'undeserving' or feckless, and for the most part leaving the latter to the mercies of the Poor Law.

However, more influential for future social work development than these attitudes and responses were some of the central principles developed by the COS, which sound surprisingly similar to those in practice today. For example, the family was to be considered as a whole; a clear parallel with family casework and even more recently with family therapy. Thorough investigation of all the circumstances and of possible sources of help was seen as essential, and this meant proper recording and oversight by case committees. Visits had to be purposeful and undertaken with the consent of the client, rather than random, wholesale or imposed. Skill and sensitivity were emphasized, qualities conspicuous by their absence in the approach of the Poor Law Officers, although they had been propounded by Thomas Chalmers in Glasgow as early as 1819. Another influential aspect of the work of the COS was the selection, training and supervision of workers. Octavia Hill acted similarly in setting up an apprenticeship scheme for her housing visitors, and she also grappled with educational dilemmas which are still current: 'how to unite the fresh, loving, spontaneous, individual sympathy with the quiet, grave, sustained and instructed spirit of the trained worker' (Woodroofe 1962: 53–4). It was the COS that first established the principle of supervision, and then, in 1896, introduced lectures and practical work in a training scheme that was eventually to become the Department of Social Science and Administration of the London School of Economics (LSE). Finally, the history of the COS exemplifies the start of a paid profession of social work. Until the 1880s, practically all the work had been done by volunteers, partly as a matter of principle – voluntary work has intrinsic value – and partly because of financial considerations. With the advent of training, however, and the greater scope for differentiating the tasks of administration, supervision and direct work, appointments of paid workers were increasingly made.

These nineteenth-century developments set the stage for the beginning of social work and, in parallel, for a climate of opinion in which the welfare state would much later become a reality. We can also begin to see clearly the impact on embryonic social work of social, political and economic trends, of legislative change, as well as of religious or philosophical thinking and value issues in society. The multiplicity of such factors, and the complexity of their interaction, have had significant influence on practice issues in present-day counselling and social work.

Social work 1900–1950

'In Britain . . . social work has from its very early days been an integral part of various statutory bodies' (Butrym 1976: 3). This was not the case with the precursors of social work before the turn of the century, when there was a sharp divide between help offered by the voluntary organizations and that provided under the Poor Law. This shift can only be explained by looking at organizational and resource issues, training developments, and not least the gradual changes in the prevailing societal beliefs about the causation of poverty and other forms of social distress.

Some specialist areas of social work were established from the beginning. This tendency towards early specialization had very significant implications for the sense of identity of social workers, their training and professional associations. It made it hard for them to see themselves as an integral part of the larger profession of social work when their main identification was with a small group with its own history and way of working. This is clearly seen in the case of the hospital almoners, one of the earliest groups to gain a distinctive identity and one with very definite parentage in the COS. In 1894, in the out-patients' department at the Royal Free Hospital, one of the COS Secretaries began to work with patients, attempting to help with their social circumstances in such a way that they would be able to benefit from their medical treatment. There was also pressure to undertake financial inquiry and prevention of fraud, but it was possible at least to establish a base for social casework in hospital and to set up some training. Other hospitals soon followed, and by 1907 a Hospital Almoners' Council, independent of the COS, was established. Training developments ensued, and a tradition of aiming for high professional standards of practice was established.

Probation has sometimes been linked with medical social work on the grounds that both types of work are based in a 'secondary setting', that is to say, a setting in which the primary purpose is not social work. Starting in 1876, police courts began to have the services of missioners, whose main function at first was to work with problems caused by drink and to promote temperance. Gradually, their remit widened to include the provision of help and guidance, to report on the home surroundings of convicted criminals, and to deal with matrimonial disputes. Legislation in 1887 and 1907 endorsed this work and created probation officers with roles not unlike those of today. Similarly, other forms of social work later grew up with both a specialist culture and with a base in state institutions, namely social work in psychiatric hospitals and in child guidance clinics. Of course, social work with deprived children had always had functions arising from poor law provision.

One of the strongest influences on social work development in the early decades of the twentieth century was a change in the

prevailing ideological climate. As long as it was believed that des-
titution and other ills were attributable only to personal failings and
individual inadequacy, then charitable measures based on the existing Victorian class structure could be seen as appropriate. However,
new awareness of structural causes of poverty gained from the social
surveys of Booth and Rowntree, coupled with new ideas about citizenship, democracy and socialism, and growing acceptance of the
idea of state welfare provision, all brought about reactions against
COS methods and the notion of charity. Corresponding shifts in
views about social work from patronage towards service also took
place. In evidence here are precursors of current struggles to establish
clients' rights, to ensure their treatment as fellow-citizens, and to
encourage their greater involvement and participation in the social
work process (Shardlow 1989; Jordan 1990).

As an important counterweight to the influence of such social
and political ideologies, and for a major contribution to the development of counselling both in its own right and as a component
of social work, we must look to insights derived from psychoanalysis. Certainly the impact of psychoanalytic thinking on social work
writing, practice and training is now more clearly perceived and
well-documented (Butrym 1976; Yelloly 1980; Pearson *et al.* 1988),
but only after much controversy – and persistent misunderstanding
on the part of some social work practitioners – has the incorporation of these insights into standard practice become acceptable.
'No topic attracts either such passionate commitment or such bitter
antagonism' (Yelloly 1980: v).

One of the handicaps of workers until after the turn of the century was their lack of knowledge of human psychology, which meant
that their meticulous observations and fact-finding could not be
fitted into a conceptual framework and understood in any depth.
However, from about 1910 onwards, Freud's ideas were beginning
to make an impact on medical psychologists and academics in London, largely as a result of the impetus provided by Dr Ernest Jones.
Psychoanalytic concepts, especially those concerning the significance
of unconscious mental processes in nervous illness, were increasingly
accepted. They were used in the psychotherapeutic treatment first
of war neuroses, then of civilian disorders. Later, their contribution to understanding in non-medical fields such as education was
acknowledged.

The early 1920s saw the gradual establishment of the 'new psychology' as it was sometimes called, a term at first understood to
include ideas from Jung and Adler, as well as Freud, especially
about the importance of the unconscious, and its implications for

treatment. The concept of the unconscious aroused enormous controversy from the beginning, and although its legitimacy is less questioned today, heated arguments about its relevance are still encountered. I will look further at the content of these arguments later, as they reflect crucial aspects of the tension between counselling concerns and the demands of social work practice.

In 1920, the Tavistock Institute of Medical Psychology was founded. This body, as the legally incorporated parent both of the post-First World War Tavistock Clinic and the post-Second World War Tavistock Institute of Human Relations, was to have a very significant impact not only on the development of social work in Britain but also on the 'social engagement of social science' internationally. The founding members of the Tavistock Group were motivated by a realization that the psychological stresses and neurotic disorders first recognized in wartime did not disappear when the war was over, but rather were an integral part of human functioning in the society which was now emerging. In order to improve understanding of these problems, a voluntary out-patient clinic was established. From the start, it combined treatment with research and teaching activities, and it valued insights from the social sciences and general medicine as well as from psychiatry and psychoanalysis. Interest focused on the then new 'dynamic psychologies' as the direction which offered most hope, and the Tavistock Clinic functioned as a mediating institution where the views of several contending parties could be aired (Trist and Murray 1990: 2).

By the 1930s, the Tavistock approach was beginning to incorporate two important features which have relevance for our concern with counselling and social work. The first of these was a readiness to question the role of social factors in psychological illness; the second was to espouse the then new 'object relations thinking' in psychoanalysis. This approach places the emphasis on relationships with significant other people rather than on instincts and drives, and explores how these external relationships are internalized and influence the development of the self and of personal identity.

Despite the ferment brought about in the medical profession by the advent of the new psychoanalytic ideas, social work itself was not much affected by these until the 1940s. A considerable amount of mythology surrounded the so-called 'psychiatric deluge', a term applied by Woodroofe (1962) to American social work between the wars, but even if it did apply there, an idea now disputed, it was not in evidence in Britain.

One development in the late 1920s which had long-term consequences for social work was the growth and influence of the child

guidance movement. Concern for children with emotional disturbances had already resulted in clinics being established in London
and Edinburgh, and this was followed by special funding being made
available to enable workers to learn from practice in the United
States, to undertake specialist training and to expand provision. An
interrelated and most influential move was the setting up in 1929
of the mental health course at the LSE. This one-year course provided a broadly based training in psychiatric social work for work
with adults, children and their families who were affected either by
psychiatric illness or mental subnormality (as it was then called).
The training included a wide range of theoretical perspectives
coupled with well-supervised fieldwork in contrasting agencies.
Probably because of the influence of the child guidance movement,
it tended to emphasize understanding of human behaviour and
relationships rather more than environmental factors, and probably
gave more weight to skills in diagnosis and direct therapy than to
those in offering material help or making practical arrangements.
Some of the psychiatric social workers thus trained were also greatly
influenced by psychoanalytic thinking, and though small in number
they made a significant impact through their writing and teaching.
On the other hand, they tended to form a somewhat envied and
distanced specialist élite, whose actual practice in psychiatric clinics
did not greatly affect the nature of work in many other social work
settings.

Apart from the developments just mentioned, the first half of the
twentieth century can be seen in retrospect as a time of stagnation
for social work, compared with the vigour and promise around
1900, and despite progess made by others in laying the foundations
of the welfare state. Practice on the whole remained at an intuitive,
commonsense level, and little was added to the existing literature.
Most of the advances in learning about the potential of social work
in the period seem to have taken place in the United States through
the application in practice, during the years of the Great Depression, of the ideas of Mary Richmond, Gordon Hamilton, Charlotte
Towle and others about how people develop and behave, how to
understand their needs, and how to influence policy and organizations to respond to them (Younghusband 1964).

What have these historical developments to tell us about the
relationship between counselling and social work? An interesting
parallel may perhaps be drawn between the situation then and our
own preoccupations today, despite the many obvious differences.
Splits between workers or agencies engaged in practical help and
those who function 'therapeutically' can be as clearly discerned

now as fifty years ago. Dilemmas of how to develop skills in relationship work, and then how to utilize them in different contexts,
are equally pertinent now as then. The insights of the child guidance movement and the mental health course at the LSE concerning fully integrated theoretical and practical learning are being
incorporated in some modern counselling courses. Similarly, this is
happening in some social work training, although at the same time
such principles are in danger of being lost, for example, in certain
modular or competence-focused courses. These issues will be taken
up again in the final chapter.

DEVELOPMENTS IN SOCIAL WORK 1950–75

This period is considerably better documented than earlier ones,
although I inevitably have to be selective in the material which
most effectively illuminates the place of counselling in social work.
As before, the complexity and the interdependence of events and
processes necessitate some general background material.

These years were a time of recognition that social problems were
so massive that action far beyond the scope of social work would
be necessary. This was despite significant improvements in the
standard of living for most people and a fairly lengthy period of full
employment. However, many remained on the margins, caught in
poverty or facing family break-up, or the vulnerability of old age,
ill-health or handicap. Demographic changes also had an impact:
medical advances resulted in elderly and handicapped people living
for longer, while earlier marriage and more mobility led to changes
in traditional family structures and support networks.

In terms of social work practice, there was an expansion in the
numbers of child care and probation officers, while those in medical
and psychiatric social work began a process of professional heart-
searching and redefinition of their roles. For example, the Institute
of Almoners pressed for a significant shift in duties away from small
administrative tasks towards casework, asserting in words which
might be part of a modern definition of counselling that their job
was:

. . . to study the patient's social background and reactions to
illness, with a view to assisting in the solution of the many personal and practical problems . . . giving help to patients where
the doctor believes their anxieties or personal difficulties are
closely associated with the illness . . . problems which require

listening, helping the patient to sort out worrying situations,
to face the future and possible readjustments to his life or the
limitations of his disability.

(Institute of Almoners 1953: 66)

Psychiatric social workers (PSWs) were grappling with somewhat different issues, such as the extent to which they should be
regarded primarily as social workers or as therapists, and how those
with a psychoanalytic orientation might use it to best advantage in
family work, group work or consultation as well as in direct work
with individuals. New forms of psychiatric treatment were beginning to bring radical alterations in both patients' needs and PSWs'
responses, with a wider range of legislative duties and more work
in the local authority mental health services.

The main advances apart from those in hospitals and clinics were
in a few specialist voluntary agencies such as the Family Service
Units and the Edinburgh Guild of Service, and in the Family Discussion Bureau (now the Institute of Marital Studies), which was
set up in 1948 by the Family Welfare Association. Such agencies,
interestingly, were places where counselling as we know it today was
practised. They focused in depth on specific social problems, system-
atically recorded and evaluated their work, undertook research, and
used innovative methods based on their growing understanding.
They also offered various training opportunities, including the chance
to develop skills and understanding in counselling at an advanced
level.

However, in the 1950s, there were still huge gaps in provision,
with little service to elderly and handicapped people, and large
workloads for the growing number of staff in the local authority
services. Although training was expanding, it could not keep pace
with the growing awareness and acknowledgement of need. Much
practice remained at a commonsense level, with little supervision,
poor record-keeping, not much cooperation, and practically no
research.

This state of affairs changed rapidly in the mid-1960s, a shift
described by Eileen Younghusband as an outburst of initiative from
many sources which heralded a new era:

something momentous happened between 1965 and 1968 which
released energies still active by 1975, in spite of massive economy
cuts. The social work profession had leapt from the margins to
the centre and was faced with a challenge to do a job to which
it had always laid claim.

(Younghusband 1978: 35)

What, then, was this momentous happening? With hindsight it is possible to discern a complex interweaving of powerful influences from a number of sources – political, legislative, organizational and professional – which taken together fundamentally altered the course of social work in the decade 1965–75. A significant increase in expenditure on the hitherto extremely patchy social services from the 1950s had led to piecemeal growth and some rather haphazard development of a number of separate small professional empires and administrative hierarchies. Emphasis on institutional provision for vulnerable children and elderly people was beginning to be replaced by concern to work preventively, intervening at an earlier stage to avoid if possible the need for residential care. Bowlby's work on the harmful effects on young children of separation from their parents and of institutional care was one influential factor in this. Demographic changes, in particular the sharp increase in the proportion of the population above pensionable age, were also affecting thinking about social policy. Expansion of services in the community, and work with families at risk, gradually came to be seen as ways forward, and legislation such as the Mental Health Act 1959 and the Children and Young Persons' Act 1963 gave backing to the different sort of work involved. The fact that people's problems spanned the areas of responsibility of several hitherto uncoordinated departments was increasingly seen as a serious obstacle to effective preventive work with families.

THE KILBRANDON AND SEEBOHM REORGANIZATIONS AND THEIR AFTERMATH

Scotland led the way in achieving the reorganization necessary for these purposes of better coordination, expansion and preventive care. Social work services there had been operating with grossly inadequate resources, but an advantage of this underdeveloped position was that when change came there was less to be disturbed and the introduction of new measures was easier. Reports of two committees of inquiry – the McBoyle Report (1963) on the Prevention of Neglect of Children and in particular the Kilbrandon Report (1964) on the shortcomings of the juvenile court system – both proposed radical changes in the entire social work system, namely a comprehensive family welfare service and a new system of children's hearings for those in need of compulsory measures of care. Social workers gave much attention to the 'matching field organization' required by the new system, and influenced central government thinking in such a way as to widen the focus from children in difficulty to all vulnerable groups in the population. The resulting legislation – the Social Work (Scotland) Act 1968 – included (unlike its later counterpart in England and Wales) the ambitious clause: 'It shall be the duty of every local authority to promote social welfare by making available advice, guidance and assistance on such a scale as may be appropriate for their area'.

Social workers themselves were now more able to see the common ground which united them as well as the distinctions between them. The formation in 1963 of the Standing Conference of Organizations of Social Workers (which later became the British Association of Social Workers) was one example of this unifying trend. This body campaigned for reform of the local authority services, in particular for their amalgamation into a single family service – 'one door on which people could knock'. Such ideas were powerfully reinforced by change in the political scene in 1964 with the new Labour government under Harold Wilson favouring increases in scale of organizations in both the private and state sectors and closer coordination between them.

This, then, was the climate of opinion in 1965 in which the Seebohm Committee was set up 'to review the organization and responsibilities of the local authority personal social services in England and Wales and to consider what changes are desirable to secure an effective family service' (Seebohm Report 1968). The committee identified very many serious shortcomings in the existing services, looked at the reasons for these, and considered various possible models for reorganization. Its recommendation was for a new department providing a community-based and family-oriented service available to all. Indeed, the hope was that it would be directed to the well-being of the whole community and not only of social casualties, a hope that in retrospect proved idealistic. A contentious issue concerned the proper place of the probation service, that is, whether it should be independent of local government control or integrated with other social work services as had happened in Scotland. In the end it was decided that it would remain a separate service for adult offenders. (Probation is discussed in detail by Brian Williams in another volume in this series, *Counselling in the Penal System*.) There was also controversy about the degree of specialization which would be appropriate in the new service; the notion that 'a family or individual in need of social care should, as far as is possible, be served by a single social worker' later caused much confusion about so-called 'generic caseloads'. Even this brief account shows that there were numerous internal contradictions in the hopes and plans.

The Social Services Act of 1970, which implemented most of the recommendations of the Seebohm Report, has undoubtedly been the most influential single piece of recent legislation in terms of its effects on the place of social work in society. Not only did this Act provide for the unification of local-authority social-work services, thus creating administrative structures of a size and complexity previously unknown to social work, but by its emphasis on total community needs and the contribution which it saw social work as making towards the meeting of these needs, it invested social work with unprecedented responsibilities.

(Butrym, 1976: 106)

It is very questionable how appropriate and feasible such global objectives were, given that the need for considerable extra resources was never sufficiently recognized. The social work task in relation to poverty and inadequate housing was not made at all clear, and Butrym believes that this situation led to unproductive guilt and wastage of workers' creative energy. She goes on to argue that another effect of the legislation was to bring about a shift in emphasis towards administration, planning and management of social provision, and that initially at least this was at the expense of the quality of social work offered at grassroots level. As many longstanding practitioners went into management positions, direct work with clients was left to the least experienced.

When the new departments came into being in 1971, major administrative restructuring was required, and for many months there was severe turbulence, even chaos, as people competed for the senior appointments, struggled with new ways of working and different colleague relationships, and tried to address newly identified unmet need. More positively, some of the major objectives, such as attracting more resources, coordinating previously fragmented services and improving client access, were in fact achieved to a limited extent after the first unsettled couple of years.

However, no sooner had a degree of stability been achieved than further massive upheaval took place. This was partly due to the reorganization of local government in England and Wales in 1974, which involved boundary changes in many authorities, with fresh appointments of chief officers and others. National Health Service (NHS) reorganization also took place in 1974, and that led to new working relationships between social services departments and health authorities. Also in 1974 (1975 in Scotland) an earlier controversial decision to transfer hospital social workers to the payroll of the local authorities was implemented. A flurry of new legislation, including the Children and Young Persons Act 1969, the Chronically Sick and Disabled Persons Act 1970, the Criminal Justice Act 1972 and the Children Act 1975, added significantly to the responsibilities of social workers, required new approaches to certain client groups, and compounded the overall sense of turbulence.

THE RECOGNITION OF CHILD ABUSE

As if all this were not enough stress for one professional group, in 1973 an event took place which was to have explosive and far-reaching consequences. This was the tragic death of Maria Colwell, aged seven, at the hands of her stepfather, after several months of violence, physical and emotional abuse and neglect. This took place while she was under social work supervision, having been fostered by an aunt, but returned to her natural mother by a court order despite Maria's extreme reluctance. The ensuing public inquiry and report (Department of Health and Social Security 1974) attracted a huge amount of media attention, most of it focused on criticisms of social work. Apart from the case of Dennis O'Neill, who was brutally killed by his foster-father in 1945, this was the first of a:

> . . . seemingly unending succession of child-care tragedies, each of which has brought in its wake attacks on the values and philosophy of social work practice and its ineffectiveness . . . The scars left by the Colwell case on the collective psyche of social work have never fully healed as each year has brought a further reminder that social work decisions are rarely clear-cut, and that social workers are brokers in shades of grey, often seeking the lesser of two evils for those with whom they work.
>
> (Bamford 1990: 4)

By 1987, there had been approximately thirty-five inquiries in child abuse. Then between 1988 and 1992 came Cleveland, Rochdale and Orkney, each concerned with sexual and even possible ritual abuse, in contrast with the physical cruelty and neglect which had been the main focus of the earlier cases. Yet again social work practice was in the spotlight, and now even more than previously there was in-depth analysis of both inter-disciplinary, inter-agency work, and of questions about direct communication with children. The significance for the counselling component in social work of this succession of child abuse inquiries is a complex matter which will be addressed in some detail in later chapters. Suffice it to say at this point that some of the inquiries:

... have been of huge public and national significance and instrumental in consolidating child maltreatment as a social problem in the U.K. [and] of critical importance in effecting a shift of resources and of the focus of work within social services departments. The exposure to public and media scrutiny provided by the inquiries and the associated fear among professionals has been a powerful catalyst for action.

(Hallett 1989: 139)

DEVELOPMENTS IN SOCIAL WORK 1975 ONWARDS

The inflation and recession of 1975 led to drastic public spending cuts and a total halt to the growth and expansion of the previous few years. These economic and political pressures meant that the already large gulf between expectations of and need for social work on the one hand, and resources to meet these on the other, became even greater. As mass unemployment once more emerged and economic growth slowed down, the large-scale bureaucratic departments came in for mounting criticism from right-wing politicians, from the media and general public, and from users of social work and social services. These attacks are partly explicable as reflecting the prejudice and stigma towards the most vulnerable and problematic sections of the community with whom social work has to an increasing extent been identified. But, additionally, the provision as set up in the early 1970s came more and more to be seen as unresponsive to need and inflexible in adapting to changing conditions and new social problems. It is perhaps not surprising that social workers were put on the defensive in the face of diametrically opposed criticisms, on the one hand that they were unnecessary, and on the other that they were failing to provide an effective safety net for the rapidly growing number of those living with unemployment, poverty and all the associated social malaise. Perhaps the industrial action which took place in 1977 and 1978 was a reaction to this. In 1979, the Conservatives came into power, and there ensued a long period of hostility to local government, reductions in public spending and rate-capping, which impinged on both social work provision and morale. A pluralist system of welfare began to be created, with support, at least in principle, for enhanced voluntary sector provision, and strong encouragement to the private sector to play a bigger role.

These shifts in public policy, taken together with all the professional questioning and heart-searching during the 1970s, made it imperative that there should be some review of the effectiveness of social work and its direction. Accordingly, the Barclay Committee was set up to 'review the role and tasks of social workers in local authority social services departments and related voluntary organizations in England and Wales and to make recommendations'. The debate occasioned by the publication of the Barclay Report in 1982 made it a highly significant milestone, not only in the recent history of social work as a whole, but also in the understanding by social workers of the place of counselling in their work. The central themes are explored at more length in subsequent chapters, but some introduction is offered here to place the report in its historical context.

One of Barclay's main assertions was that social work comprises two major activities – counselling and social care planning – the latter being understood as both direct and indirect work to solve or alleviate existing problems and to prevent future social problems. These two activities, it concluded, 'are not performed only by social workers but all who call themselves social workers must be able to carry out both' (Barclay 1982: 51).

There was, however, dissension among the members of the Barclay working party about the most appropriate model of service delivery. The majority advocated a 'community social work approach', based on close working partnerships with citizens and an attitude of mind which acknowledges and values the care given by networks of informal relationships in the community, and which aims to support and strengthen these caring networks. One minority note made the case for a more radical variant of this orientation, namely 'neighbourhood-based social work', which would mean the evolution of new, decentralized structures with primary social care teams in every locality. A second minority note put forward 'an alternative view' of particular relevance for our present concern with counselling. In this, Pinker advocated a less radical, more cautious reform and reasserted the role of 'social casework' as the distinctive process and method of intervention of social workers, not necessarily their chief activity but an essential part of their work.

These dissensions in the Barclay Report portray very vividly a dichotomy in thinking about social work practice which was much in evidence in the 1970s and which has strongly persisted ever since. This may be expressed as a battle between two views: one, that social work is professionalized casework (a near equivalent of counselling), and two, the notion that social work is predominantly about community involvement and political action. The pendulum has swung between these two extremes at various points in the last forty years, often with much unproductive rhetoric between those in opposing factions who have generally failed to recognize any validity in the opposing view. And now, in the 1990s, that pendulum is swinging again, with consequences for the counselling dimension of the work which as yet cannot be clearly foreseen.

This continuing argument within social work practice can be seen as a close parallel with the wider debates about the overall relationship between social work and counselling. In both arenas, there is reluctance to acknowledge that each type of approach is needed, and to see the potential complementarity between them. There is some readiness to see that a degree of common ground exists, and yet it is extremely difficult to define precisely the areas of overlap and to perceive their implications for practice. It is equally difficult for those involved in one field to avoid invidious comparisons with the other, leading to professional jealousies and stereotyping. A polarizing process is thus set in train which squanders workers' energies and makes it less likely that those in need will get the resources they so badly want.

This current dichotomy vividly sets the scene for the context of counselling in social work and hence provides a fitting introduction to the next chapter.

· TWO ·

The context of counselling in social work

The historical and developmental survey in Chapter One brought us to the point where an uneasy polarization between counselling and social work could be discerned. Some of the reasons for this, and the practical implications of it, can only be understood by exploring the impact of the various types of environments in which these activities are located. The aim in this chapter is therefore to clarify the nature and significance of 'context' in general, and to convey the complexity of social work as one specific context for the practice of counselling.

WHAT IS CONTEXT AND WHY IS IT IMPORTANT?

The word 'context' derives from a Latin word meaning 'to weave together', and may be defined as 'parts that precede or follow a word or passage and contribute to its full meaning, or, the conditions or circumstances that are relevant to an event, fact, etc.' (Collins 1991). The image of weaving strands together fits well, especially as it implies not only what comes before and after, but also what is alongside, currently influencing and being influenced by the subject. But how do we ascertain what factors are significant, relevant and truly interactive and influential as opposed to being simply concurrent? And how do we assign the appropriate amount of impact, neither too much or too little? These questions themselves reflect the process of assessment in counselling and social work, where tentative guesses are made by the worker as to what might be the most meaningful links to be explored. In such matters, it is tempting to allow ourselves to be blinkered and fail to perceive important areas of relevance, rather than grapple with the complexities that a more inclusive approach involves.

The growth of professional practice is only understandable against a background of general societal change – that is, demographic factors, major global events such as world wars, economic recessions, technological advances, changes in employment patterns, health care, standards of living, modes of communication, and the trend away from stability resulting in turbulence. Changes in these areas, which of course interact with each other, in turn affect and are affected by cultural factors such as values, ideologies and expectations. A contextual perspective fully acknowledges this increasing interdependence of different aspects of our society: 'no man is an island'.

Systems thinking (Emery 1969) is a conceptual framework that encompasses ideas of wholeness, organization and dynamic interaction, as opposed to compartmentalizing phenomena or roughly amalgamating them. This framework places emphasis on the interrelationships and interactions of the parts of a whole, namely the system, its environment or supra-system and its components or sub-systems, seen in hierarchical terms. The notion that a whole is more than the sum of its parts is central to this approach and is used in both the natural and social sciences. Another fundamental concept is the notion of boundary – that which divides the subject from its surrounding world, and permits certain elements to enter while restricting the exchange of other materials. A boundary which is too permeable results in loss of identity, whereas a boundary which is closed or impermeable leads to atrophy and death. This notion helps us to distinguish between 'open' and 'closed' systems, which are valuable metaphors for individual and societal human functioning.

Human organizations are living systems, and can be understood as 'open systems' in the sense of being open to exchange with their environments:

> an open system, of whatever size, demonstrates exploratory behaviour, is adaptable, creative, confident, and takes in and acts fruitfully upon new information . . . It allows considerable autonomy for its members. Its boundaries are, therefore, flexible rather than impermeable and fixed. Its face is not set against change.
>
> (Preston-Shoot and Agass 1990: 49)

The emphasis on transactions across boundaries, such as communication, is an important feature of systems thinking. Understanding of family transactions and of organizational dynamics are particularly relevant in the context of counselling in social work. It is from the field of family therapy that these ideas have had most influence on social work practice. Organizational commentators and consultants (Bridger 1981; Menzies-Lyth 1988, 1989; Ambrose 1989) have also integrated such systems thinking with psychoanalytic concepts in their work on the management of change in organizational life. Bridger's 'transitional approach to the management of change' is a useful way of looking at relevance to changing patterns of social work practice:

> If organisations and communities are to maintain their health in rapidly-changing environments, an open-system perspective is essential on the part of those who manage change within them. Such a perspective recognises not only the interdependence of the different parts that make up the organisation as a whole system but also the exposure and vulnerability of the whole to environmental forces impinging on it. To a much greater extent than ever before managements now have to reconcile institutional needs with those outside forces. Coping with the ailments afflicting an organisation is different from coping with those affecting the individuals who comprise it. Internal malfunctioning and conflicts, whether of individuals or groups, can no longer be managed as if in a closed-system. They have now to be seen in the context of the wider environment of the organisation with all its complexity, uncertainty and unpredictability.
>
> (Ambrose 1989: 148)

This statement reinforces Emery's (1969) view that just because environmental interactions are forbiddingly complex does not mean that we have any excuse to isolate organizations conceptually.

One important element of this complexity, and an essential characteristic of the world we inhabit, is turbulence, and I believe it is important to look at this before discussing the specific influence of politics, public opinion, legislation and organizational structure on the practice of counselling in social work. By 'turbulence' I mean the unpredictable, risky, tension-ridden and extremely stressful nature of our environment, with its apparently escalating violence, and a sense of things being out of control. Wars, famine, depletion of the earth's resources and the AIDS epidemic are global examples, and they have domestic parallels. What we sometimes overlook is the impact of all this not just on individuals, but also on the functioning and interactions of institutions and professional groups. If a sense of stability is diminished or lost altogether, and if assumptions about basic values are increasingly questioned, then there is a level of confusion, pain, threat and anxiety to which policy makers and practitioners as well as service users must be subject. The greater the degree of anxiety in relation to one's tolerance and ability to manage it, the more will there be a need to construct defences against it as protection against the worst aspects of the situation. Illustrations of such defensive strategies include denial, flight, scapegoating, splitting and projection, and idealization. The problem with such defences is that while in the short term they serve as an essential means of surviving and coping, in the longer term they perpetuate barriers to effective functioning and to constructive relationships between people, not only personally, but also at the organizational level. The processes surrounding investigations into child abuse, including the common tendency to blame the social worker, provide a recurrent example of these dynamics which will be discussed in detail later. I believe that understanding in depth of such 'internal' dynamics as these is as important as the analysis of the apparently more rational or practical 'external' factors.

THE CURRENT SOCIETAL CONTEXT

However, focusing now on the external environment of modern British society, we see that tension and anxiety, change and diversity are all characteristic features, which inevitably have great influence on the work of the caring professions.

We live at a time when unemployment has reached almost unprecedented levels, when problems of poverty and homelessness are seemingly intractable, and when the gap between rich and poor is widening markedly. A few statistics illustrate this. According to government figures, the numbers of people living on less than half the average level of income more than doubled in the ten years up to 1988–89. In 1988, the poorer 50 per cent owned 6 per cent of marketable wealth (*Social Trends* 1991). In 1987, almost a fifth of the population were living in poverty (at or below supplementary benefit level). The numbers of those living in bed and breakfast accommodation or in hostels, in squats or on the streets had increased very dramatically by the early 1990s, as had house repossessions due to inability to keep up mortgage repayments.

We live in a multiracial, culturally diverse society, and sadly one in which despite various efforts there exist very serious problems of both individual and institutional racism, that is to say, a belief in the inherent superiority of one race over another, and therefore the right to dominate and exploit those ethnic groups assumed to be inferior. There are thought to be between 2 and 2.5 million people in Britain whose ethnic origins are in the New Commonwealth and Pakistan, and of these perhaps half are British-born. They comprise around 5 per cent of the population, while a further 5 per cent or so is made up other significant ethnic groups such as Chinese, Greek Cypriots and Jews. The greatest degree of prejudice and stereotyping tends to be perpetrated against 'black' people, those of Asian, African and Caribbean descent.

Great inequality, injustice and discrimination thus persist in modern Britain, both in the way it is run, and in how its resources are doled out; people's life chances are to a large extent determined by skin colour, gender, class and age:

It is no coincidence that the vast majority of 'heavy-end' clients are poor, and that poor areas produce higher rates of all social problems than wealthier ones. Nor is it any coincidence that black people are over-represented in the proportions of people in prisons and children in care, and under-represented among people using resources which clients see as helpful and desirable. Nor yet is it a coincidence that women provide disproportionate numbers of social workers' most needy clients – especially single parents and people with mental health problems. All these facts reflect the way power is used by better-off white males, and the advantages and disadvantages that accrue from unequal holdings of assets in British society.

(Jordan 1990: 5)

These assertions powerfully convey some of the consequences for help-seekers of certain aspects of present-day society. Many if not most clients are casualties of the sort of turbulence described earlier, the accelerating economic and technological changes and social upheaval which interact very significantly with people's psychological well-being or otherwise. The assertions also give pointers to the ways that social work practice, including its counselling dimension, are affected, a debate which I will return to in Chapter Three. As Kwhali (1991: 41) states: 'Issues of control, containment, inequality and oppression are central not simply to the social worker's daily tasks, but to the wider organizational and societal context within which social work is located'.

THE USE AND PROVISION OF SOCIAL WORK

Who requires social work? One possible starting point in attempting to answer this question would be to identify the range of needs experienced by people in our society today, and then to select from those the ones which social work is equipped to meet. A rough list of needs might encompass the following:

- Universal human need, e.g. for food and shelter.
- Needs affected by structural change in society, or by emerging social problems, such as unemployment or HIV/AIDS.
- Needs contingent upon specific personal situations or relationships, e.g. those arising from physical or mental illness or handicap, marital disharmony, child sexual abuse.
- Needs resulting from unforeseen calamities such as major disasters.

Although such a catalogue seems informative and useful at first sight, could the task of social work really be defined as the meeting of such needs? Perlman (1973), in advocating a problem-focused rather than a needs-focused approach, criticizes such a 'needs list' for being too vaguely defined, for encouraging the illusion that social workers can be all things to all people all the time, and for risking too great a fragmentation of scarce resources. By contrast, her problem-centred approach is much more deliberately and selectively focused on clearly identified problems, felt and seen by those involved, which are then addressed by tasks agreed upon by both client and worker. Although Perlman was discussing social casework as it was practised in the 1970s, these ideas were generally influential and have imbued much of social work practice today. Her definitions usefully highlight some issues we need to address in analysing the place of counselling in social work:

> casework is a problem-solving process by which an individual (or family group) is helped to cope more effectively and gratifyingly with some problematic aspect(s) of his person-to-task or person-to-person roles ('to cope with', not 'to adjust to').
>
> (Perlman 1973: 11)

She identifies three reasons for the breakdown in people's ability to cope with such roles:

- Actual deficits of means by which to cope.
- Discrepancies of various sorts causing people to be thwarted, blocked or confused about how to cope.
- Disturbances or distortions of emotion, thought and/or behaviour.

Similar ideas are expressed in a more down-to-earth way in the Barclay Report (1982), when it speaks of the far-reaching functions and powers given by Parliament to social services authorities to provide help to people with practical, emotional and behavioural problems.

THE LOCATION OF SOCIAL WORK

This mention of the statutory powers given to a certain type of department highlights the question of where social workers are located. The function of the agency and its location within its environment have immense significance for the nature of the relationship of practitioner to user and hence for the nature of the work done.

Local authorities

Social work provision in the main has to be seen as part of the wider social services remit of local authorities, which in turn depends on social policy and political decision at both central and local government levels. Very many Acts of Parliament provide the legal boundaries within which social workers must function. This applies even to those working in the voluntary sector, to the extent that their agency functions as an agent of the local authority in its service provision.

The vast majority of social workers have, since the 1970s, been employed by local authorities in large-scale welfare bureaucracies. These are the social services departments (social work departments in Scotland), whose primary functions are contained in legislation. They are financed from central and local government sources and run by a director who is accountable for service provision to a committee of elected Council members. This public accountability is an important element in determining the amount and type of social work provision which can be made available. The probation service is another locally administered social work service, whose workers are officers of the courts working mainly with offenders and their families. In England and Wales, it is financed entirely by central government and functions quite separately from the social services departments, whereas in Scotland the service has been provided as an integral part of the work of the local authority social work departments. (Probation is covered in another volume in this series, *Counselling in the Penal System*, by Brian Williams.)

Any blanket statement about the local authority employment base of social workers (probably about 90 per cent of all in practice) does not do justice, however, to the great diversity of settings in which they are deployed. These include teams responsible for a defined geographical area, teams catering for a specific client group or those engaged in a particular way of working – specialist projects, residential and day-care units, and attachments to hospitals, health centres, schools or prisons.

The setting has an important influence on the weighting of various types of activity, such as the amount and nature of collaborative work with people in other disciplines, the extent of long-term involvement with clients, and the balance between responding to crises and attempting some preventive work. It also determines the degree of authorization given to social workers to prioritize particular areas of work and to allocate resources.

Voluntary organizations

About 10 per cent of social workers practise in voluntary organizations, where there is possibly even greater diversity than in the public sector. Some voluntary organizations, such as Barnardo's, are large-scale, nationwide and of long standing; others are very small, community-based and recently established. Their activities may overlap to a considerable extent with the statutory departments, but their opportunities and constraints will be very different, as will the emphasis placed on particular areas of work and on the way it is carried out. In general, voluntary organizations are seen as having more flexibility. Their funding is likely to be derived from trust funds and charitable donations as well as from grants and fees for services from local authority and central government sources. Their management is equally diverse, ranging from hierarchies not unlike those in the local authority to small, relatively informal committees of volunteers. Social workers move fairly easily between the two systems, and their career progression in each is similar.

The Barclay Report (1982) helpfully identified a range of roles which voluntary social work organizations may well be able to fulfil to a greater degree than local authorities. These roles include acting as a watchdog or critical observer, sometimes engaging in conflict with statutory departments and pressing for change. Another potential role, clearly seen in the history of social provision, is that of specialist, able to focus quite narrowly on the needs of particular users, such as those coping with a specific physical disability or, more recently, members of particular ethnic groups. This role may in turn offer opportunities to engage in primary prevention, forestalling trouble by creating the conditions in which it is less likely to arise. Many voluntary organizations came into being to pioneer new ways of working or to explore areas of unmet need. This innovative role remains very significant even when the local authority can share it, and it is a vital contribution when the weight of statutory responsibilities is such that the local authority is forced to restrict its help to some sectors of the population quite rigorously.

Private practice

A very tiny minority of social workers are found in the private sector, as hitherto there has been no insurance system, whether state or private, for paying a self-employed worker, and no significant infrastructure for linking workers and clients. Nor has there been a formal licensing system to which those in private practice could be accountable. Now the numbers of such workers are slowly increasing, especially as sessionally paid workers in independent agencies, as freelance trainers, or as guardians *ad litem* in the child care field. In most instances, the nature of their work is significantly different from that of mainstream social work, and may involve extra training. Interestingly, those who move into private work tend to use titles like 'counsellor' or 'consultant' rather than 'social worker', perhaps reflecting an implicit but widely held view of status differentials.

THE POLITICAL AND LEGAL CLIMATE OF SOCIAL WORK

Because social work's location is largely within the services of the state, it must largely reflect the most prevalent political attitudes towards the social problems it is intended to address. Political ideologies change over time, and some major shifts in social work provision are attributable to such changes. Social workers themselves, however, are not uncritical or unquestioning in their implementation of politically determined policies. Clement Attlee said in 1920 that every social worker is almost certain to be an agitator.

Especially from the late 1960s onwards, social workers have been embroiled to varying degrees in political debate with each other and with their employers. Radical and Marxist perspectives were influential in such debate, highlighting the social control and coercive aspects of social work, and the implicit tendency to blame people personally for problems which have social origins, thus isolating them from the support of others in similar circumstances. The ferment to which such ideological battles gave rise, coinciding as they did with the retrenchment of services and resources in the mid-1970s, highlighted the degree to which social workers are caught between, on the one hand, those with the greatest degree of control and, on the other, the most powerless and vulnerable groups in our society. This period saw social workers, especially younger ones employed in inner-city areas, involved in protests and strikes, campaigning both on behalf of their oppressed clients and also for better conditions and recognition of their own needs. They had to acknowledge their own political position and its implications more explicitly than ever before.

Several consequences followed. One was a heightened aware-ness of the necessity for social workers to have a negotiating role, both with their clients and on their clients' behalf. Another was the trend away from paternalistic attitudes to those in difficulty, coupled with an increasing emphasis on notions like participation, clients as fellow citizens, openness and self-help, which are cur-rently much debated and very usefully enacted. These ideas will be explored further in Chapter Three. A further result of the politic-ization of social work was a tendency to neglect the psychological component of human problems in favour of structural explana-tions, leading to unfortunate polarization of approaches to com-bat the difficulty. Casework, psychodynamic ideas, counselling and therapeutic approaches in general all attracted more hostility than previously, to the extent that both in legislation and in actual practice there was and still is a serious risk of abandoning them entirely.

In terms of the legal climate, the question arises of whether the law is a context of social work or its *raison d'être*. The immense significance of this question for the nature of counselling in social work is highlighted in a seminal discussion of child protection, the law and dangerousness (Parton and Parton 1989). Some background material on trends in public concern about child abuse is necessary before focusing on the ways in which the legal framework influ-ences or determines social work practice.

Maria Colwell's death in 1973 was referred to in Chapter One as marking the start of what for social work has now become its great-est preoccupation – the central concern for child protection. The sequence of committees of inquiry into the abuse of children (around forty between 1973 and 1993) has done more than anything else to influence public and political opinion on the issue, and thus radically to alter the professional response of social workers and of many other practitioners in the health and welfare field. To begin with, from the late 1960s to the early 1980s, ignorance and emotional reluctance tended to result in non-recognition of the problem of child abuse and insufficient intervention in situations of risk. 'Battered babies' and then 'non-accidental injury' were the labels used at first. Only later were emotional cruelty, neglect and failure to thrive defined as abuse. It was not until the 1980s that sexual abuse began to be fully acknowledged and worked with, and there is still only very limited understanding of the nature and extent of ritualistic abuse. 'Child abuse' is now the global term for these various forms of victimization of children, but from a professional standpoint the phrase 'protection of children at risk' is the most helpful in indicating the central task and in emphasizing that the child is the main focus.

At the same time as the whole concept of child abuse was widening, so too was the degree of public awareness of the problem. This can be seen for example in the fact that Childline, a telephone counselling service for children in trouble or danger, was, according to its June 1993 Factsheet, answering 2700 calls out of around 10,000 attempted calls each day. The huge amount of media coverage of the Butler-Sloss inquiry into child abuse in Cleveland in 1988 and also of the events in Orkney in 1991–92 is further evidence of public interest. In these two cases, and also to a lesser extent in Rochdale, the main criticisms were not to do with insufficient intervention by professional workers, but too much, and in particular the unwarranted intrusion upon families and removal of children on the basis of inadequate evidence. In consequence, the expectations and pressures on social workers are changing in intensity and growing in volume.

The contradictory requirements now placed by society upon social workers seem to imply that they must prevent any children suffering serious harm at the hands of their parents, without ever taking action that is delayed or over-hasty, or indeed making any mistakes in identification and treatment. Yet it is manifestly impossible for any one profession alone to assess accurately either the extent of existing abuse or the degree of future risk. Furthermore, it is not readily acknowledged that some tragedies, by the very nature of the covert cultures in which they develop, simply cannot be prevented. Even if standards of research, training, supervision, multidisciplinary collaboration and resource provision doubled overnight, the vagaries of human nature, societal stress and the inherently risky nature of critical decision making would still combine to result in death or severe emotional trauma for some children – less common maybe, but never totally eliminated.

Urgent questions about the relationship of social work with the law were raised in especially acute form by reports of inquiry into the deaths in 1985 and 1987 of three children – Jasmine Beckford, Kimberley Carlile and Tyra Henry. The first of these reports, in a statement which also looks at assumptions about the counselling dimension in social work, emphasizes the public accountability of social workers, suggesting that they themselves had not hitherto appreciated the extent of this:

> The academic origins of modern social work in the 1950s case-work literature had led many to believe that the one-to-one therapeutic relationship was at the heart of professional social work practice . . . We are strongly of the view that social work can, in fact, be defined only in terms of the functions required of its practitioners by their employing agency operating within a statutory framework.
>
> (Beckford Report 1985: 12)

Parton and Parton (1989: 56) point out that this is tantamount to arguing:

> . . . that the crucial element which provides modern social work with its rationale and legitimacy is its relationship with the law . . . Social work, then, can not only be understood within its legal framework but, in effect, social work activity is the functioning of the law in practice.

To the extent that this legal imperative of social work is true in practice, there are profound consequences for any counselling role in social work. Child protection is only one of many tasks which requires social workers to adopt a policing or surveillance role. Compulsory detention in hospital of mentally disordered persons (Mental Health Act 1983; Mental Health (Scotland) Act 1984) provides another example. Yet another is the complex balancing of rights and risks in relation to very confused elderly people living alone at home. The apprehension, unease and anxiety felt by social workers towards such demands for more formalized responses can be expressed very eloquently in the form of a dilemma:

> . . . when child abuse is suspected, there may follow a radical change in the one-to-one relationship with the client: what was seen as a helping, supportive role may now be perceived as punitive and authoritarian . . . Can the social worker fulfil a policing role, firmly and efficiently, if he has also to gain the

family's confidence, and to convey the personal warmth and
genuineness necessary for him to provide the support which
will enable them to become better parents?

(Beckford Report 1985: 15)

A slightly different perspective on the same issue is expressed in
a trenchant critique of the way that the law during the 1980s tended
to become an institution for determining child welfare issues: 'It is
disturbing when social workers seem more anxious to learn about
court procedures, legal strategies, rules of evidence and how to give
a good performance in court than about child development and the
most effective ways of helping families' (King and Trowell 1992: 7).

To what degree must and should social workers function as agents
of the state? Is it possible for them to reconcile such a position with
a valid counselling role? Do they possess an identity separate from
the law, even though their work is influenced and bounded by it?
These are vital questions which will recur throughout this book.

MEDIA PRESSURE

Exploration in depth of the influence of the media on any social
institution is a complex topic ouside the scope of this book. However, media pressure seems to be an increasingly significant factor
in responses by politicians, policy makers and practitioners to child
abuse and to other social problems in which social workers are
seen as having a central role. It is not surprising, and indeed it is
entirely appropriate, that when a tragedy or scandal takes place it
should be a matter of public concern. Examples of ill-treatment
of elderly patients in hospital, abuse of youngsters in residential
care, and deaths of young children in their own homes raise serious
questions: What went wrong? How did this come about? Who is
to blame? How can similar occurrences be prevented? In many
situations, media reports have served a valuable function in identifying a specific problem, ensuring it is taken seriously, and raising the general level of public awareness about the wider issues.
However, this positive function requires a degree of understanding
and impartiality which cannot be assumed in all sections of the
media. It is where scandal-mongering or profit become the primary
motives for reporting an event that much damage is likely to be
done. Even benign forms of media coverage may carry risks or lead
to unintended negative outcomes. Some of the risks are immediate
and self-evident, such as the greatly increased distress caused by

extra publicity to those already suffering from an incident. Other forms of damage may be more insidious and have long-term consequences, and it is this sort of influence which is having particular impact on social work and ultimately on the place of counselling within it.

Focusing on the particular example of child abuse inquiries, Hallett (1989) discusses the pros and cons of holding these in public or in private. Issues of national importance when there is a major crisis of public confidence would probably constitute the main reason for a public inquiry. The advantages of holding an inquiry in private, as was recommended by the Department of Health and Social Security (DHSS) in 1985, include not only the likelihood of securing the voluntary cooperation of witnesses and encouraging them to speak freely, but also lessening the risk of injustice through media reporting of evidence before those affected have had a chance to rebut it. Hallett also shows how both local media campaigns and the reporting of criminal trials have resulted in pressure for an independent inquiry. Widely reported criticisms of professional behaviour by judges at criminal trials have been known to both pre-empt and to be at odds with the findings of a later inquiry.

A now familiar tendency of media reportage of the findings of public inquiries has been to focus attention on the inadequacy or failure of named individual workers. Most often a particular social worker has been singled out by the press for the harshest criticism, regardless of how many other agencies, professional workers or tiers of management were thought by the panel of inquiry to have shared responsibility for the tragedy. This tendency to set in train a scapegoating process, with consequent loss of morale and confidence on the part of social workers, is one of the most destructive impacts of media involvement. Perhaps even more damaging in the long term is the way it has shaped the image of social work held by clients and potential users of the service. Some of the most vulnerable and isolated parents now fear social workers: 'If they come, it will be to take my child away!' is the widely held view. This suspicion distances those in need from much of the support they should have a right to expect. A less evident but equally far-reaching outcome can be seen in the organizational reactions of departments employing social workers. Some collude with the generally held denial of the extreme complexity of the work and tend to produce very rigid, categorical guidelines for practice, aimed more at proving that the work is procedurally correct than at enabling good practice. This buttresses a trend away from therapeutic responses to troubled families, in favour of a more inspectorial approach akin to social policing, in which it is not possible to let clients take all the responsibility for themselves, and at the same time reduces their anonymity. The counselling aspect of the work is thus seriously marginalized.

THE IMPACT OF THE BARCLAY AND GRIFFITHS REPORTS ON SOCIAL WORK PRACTICE

The shape of social work has been affected not only by public inquiries but also by successive government reports and resultant legislation. In particular, the place of counselling within it has been affected by these forces more than has any other arena of counselling. The influence of such reports on social work delivery and practice has been and will continue to be so massive and far-reaching, that they constitute in effect the single most powerful determinant of the context of counselling in social work. The Seebohm Report has already been discussed as part of the historical introduction in Chapter One. Here, the focus is on the Barclay and Griffiths Reports, because these have the most relevance for our contextual theme.

The Barclay Report

The starting point of this report was the explication of confusion and conflict especially as experienced by social workers in defining their role and tasks:

> Too much is generally expected of social workers. We load upon them unrealistic expectations and we then complain when they do not live up to them ... Social workers find it difficult to come to terms with the complex pressures which surround them. There is confusion about the direction in which they are going and unease about what they should be doing and the way in which they are organised and deployed. When things go wrong the media have tended to blame them because it is assumed that their job is to care for people so as to prevent trouble arising. They operate uneasily on the frontier between what appears to be almost limitless needs on the one hand and an inadequate pool of resources to satisfy those needs on the other.
>
> (Barclay 1982: vii)

In exploring what social workers are needed to do, the Barclay Report identified two different but interlocking activities: social care planning and counselling. The first of these, *social care planning*, involves planning, establishing, maintaining and evaluating the provision of social care, at all levels from the wide geographical area to the individual family. It includes discovering existing networks and creating new ones, ascertaining the needs and views of those in the locality, formulating policy, setting up facilities, negotiating with other agencies, encouraging self-help, the use of volunteers and community initiatives, and monitoring the results. This developmental sort of activity is seen by Barclay as a complex skilled task, not to be dismissed as some people had, 'as "work with the environment" or "work with other than the client" as if client and environment were not part of an inseparable interacting universe with built-in capacities for mutual support and help' (Barclay 1982: 39).

The second activity in Barclay's scheme, *counselling*, is defined as the process of direct communication and interaction between clients and social workers, through which clients are helped to change, or to tolerate, some aspects of themselves or of their environment. It is later defined specifically as a range of activities in which an attempt is made to understand the meaning of some event or state of being to an individual, family or group and to plan, with the person or people concerned, how to manage the emotional and practical realities which face them (Barclay 1982: xiv, 41).

In the Barclay Report's second minority note (Appendix B: 'An alternative view'), Professor R.A. Pinker enlarged on his view of a revised 'social casework' as the way forward. He quoted Yelloly's (1980) description of social casework as a method of work which takes account not only of the personal but also the social aspects of human problems, which are so severe that they threaten or destroy clients' capacity to manage their own lives or to function effectively as members of society. Pinker included both counselling and practical tasks in his definition, and saw the counselling component as 'carried out through the use of a professional relationship between the social worker and the client (and other people who are immediately affected) as the means of helping the client to manage his own life' (Barclay 1982: 239).

Pinker strongly criticized both the main report and the other minority report (Appendix A, by Brown, Hadley and White). The latter proposed that social workers should be based in 'patch teams' in every locality, and should possess a thorough grounding in work with families having children at risk and with elderly people. In addition, they would be skilled in preventive measures, the development of voluntary and self-help organizations and in working at second-hand through lay people. They would be able to call on specialist workers to deal with specific client groups such as people with mental health problems, but overall their orientation would be more generalist, and also more informal and less narrowly professional. Counselling skills would have a much less central place in their work. Pinker's criticisms of these ideas included doubts about the concept of 'community', lack of adequate analysis of accountability issues, the danger of relegating specialist work to the margins, the threat to people's right to privacy and confidentiality implicit in community and neighbourhood models, and the problem of incorporating all the new ideas into training programmes without vastly increasing their duration.

Pinker's serious concern about the political implications of some of these proposals act as a strong reminder of the way in which social work has to contend with ideological conflicts in any attempt to define and organize its provision. Many of the themes in the Barclay Report have continued to preoccupy social workers ever since its publication.

Community care

The Griffiths Report (1988), *Community Care: Agenda for Action*, together with the White Paper *Caring for People* (Department of Health 1989) and subsequent community care legislation contained in the NHS and Community Care Act 1990, can be seen as continuing to address the issues of social care planning debated in the Barclay Report. The dilemmas of trying to bring together the dual concerns of broad policy development and the needs of individuals, families and groups are also highlighted. Although social workers as such are mentioned very rarely in the community care documents cited, the implications of the legislation for their role and the way they work are immense and far-reaching.

Community care – the enabling of people to live as independently as possible in their own homes – has long been a worthy aspiration, but little consensus has existed about its meaning and application to different vulnerable groups. The most vulnerable include elderly and disabled people, those with a mental handicap and those who are mentally ill. As well as regarding care at home rather than in institutions as more humane, there has been a naive assumption by 'society' that it is a much cheaper option. Politicians, policy makers and the general public have also been greatly confused about the distinction between 'care in the community' and 'care by the community'. A consequence of these assumptions and confusions has, according to many observers (Finch and Groves 1983; Ungerson 1985; Hanmer and Statham 1988), been a tendency to exploit informal primary carers, particularly women, by failing to acknowledge the magnitude of the burden on them and leaving them without adequate resources or support.

Sir Roy Griffiths was asked by the Secretary of State for Social Services 'to review the way in which public funds are used to support community care policy and to advise on the options for action'. Griffiths saw the tasks of publicly provided services as being, first, to support and strengthen existing networks of carers – families, friends, neighbours – and, second, to identify where these have broken down or cannot meet the needs, and to decide what public services might fill the gap. It is the means by which these tasks should be carried out which constitute the most radical change to the *status quo*. Instead of the social services authorities themselves being the chief providers of care, they should assess need and design, organize, purchase and deliver services within the finite resources available. They are expected to make maximum use of voluntary and private sector bodies, thus developing a 'mixed welfare economy'.

Most of the debate about these proposals was concerned with the likely inadequacy of available resources to meet increased expectations. Less thoroughly discussed were the fundamental changes in the roles and relationships of the workers faced with implementing the ideas. Although social workers are not the only professionals to assume responsibility for the new functions, they are seen as among the most suitable because of their regular contact with clients. The role of 'case manager' is especially pertinent to the counselling component of social work. As described in the White Paper, this role involves taking 'responsibility for ensuring that individuals' needs are regularly reviewed, resources are managed effectively and that each service user has a single point of contact' (Department of Health 1989: 3.3.2). For workers accustomed to being direct providers, nothing less than a complete transformation of their role and a massive culture shift is involved. Instead of making an objective assesssment of need, they are having to become rationers of resources, with new budgetary duties, concerned with cost-efficiency, monitoring and gatekeeping.

In taking on their new responsibilities social work staff will be building on existing skills but their training will need to reflect their new roles in developing local authority community care plans, in procuring and commissioning services and in

implementing individual care programmes with professional and
financial oversight.

(Department of Health 1989: 10.12)

IMPLICATIONS FOR COUNSELLING

What implications do such roles have for counselling and the client–
worker relationship? Biggs (1991) points out that the concept of
case management assumes a marketplace model of interpersonal
relationships, in which two equal individuals come together to
agree a bargain on the exchange of goods and services. He goes
on to identify a number of crucial gaps in this assumption; namely,
that it sees the relationships as unproblematic and unconflictual,
that processes leading up to and following the point of transaction
are not addressed, that the situation is viewed as predominantly
rational, with little concern about underlying motivations, and that
the context and allegiances of the specific individual are neglected.
A conflict of interest may well exist between the client and informal carer, who, if within a husband–wife or parent–child relationship, could be working through long-standing tensions as well as
the current care problem. This complex reality cannot be addressed
properly in a system geared predominantly to economy, technical
efficiency and rationality. It is too early to predict exactly how these
dilemmas will be managed in practice, but what already seems clear
is that face-to-face work in depth with distressed individuals and
their carers is not compatible with case management.

Where, in the light of these developments, might counselling find
an appropriate place in social work practice? Bamford (1990) pro-
poses a logical organizational response to the dual contradictory
demands faced by social workers; namely, the mismatch between
societal expectations and the aspirations of social work and, in
addition, the conflict between the role of gatekeeper to the allocation of resources and that of counsellor and advocate. Bamford's
idea is to divide the workload into three separate categories, clearly
distinguishing the tasks of social work from social care (including
case management) on the one hand, and from service planning,
monitoring and policy evaluation on the other. This division recog-
nizes that very different skills are needed for each of these activities, and that social work is not the only occupational group able
to undertake the latter two. He suggests that the social work service would use a variety of counselling skills to work with those
mainly needing a therapeutic approach to cope with loss, change
and adaptation. Social work is here viewed as:

> ... a relationship between worker and client in which social
> workers attempt to help clients whose difficulties are so severe
> that they threaten their capacity to manage their own lives or
> to function effectively as members of society, and through use
> of that relationship assist clients to a better understanding of
> their problems and their own capabilities to bring about change,
> if necessary mobilising community resources to facilitate the
> process of change.
>
> (Bamford 1990: 162)

One important question to consider in the context of counselling
issues is the impact on direct practice of social work's location in
large local government bureaucracies. Indeed, it could be argued
that a most important consequence for counselling practice is the
powerful tension experienced by workers between the very personal nature of the tasks being undertaken and the impersonal
nature of the bureaucratic and legislative framework. Many commentators have pointed out how following the Seebohm changes
in the early 1970s there was a strong sense that the centralized,
remote nature of the organization powerfully militated against
the personal nature of the social work task. Research in a deprived
inner-city area (Satyamurti 1981) demonstrated how quickly the
then new departments came to be viewed by workers in other state
departments, notably but by no means exclusively supplementary benefits officers, as the place to which they could refer their
unwanted or marginal cases. The same study indicated that social
workers did not easily identify with their own department, viewing
it as a source of frustration or, at best, devoid of meaning. The
relationships of social workers with their own higher management
were inevitably distant in what Jordan (1984: 110) described as
'a large organisation staffed by young, disaffected and relatively
inexperienced workers, under the close administrative control of a
large hierarchy of well-organised bureaucrats and confused, alien-
ated, senior professionals, bemoaning their lack of contact with
clients'. The massive scale of operations made it more likely that
clients would be considered and treated outside their social context.

In a controversial paper entitled 'The post-Seebohm depression',
Woodmansey (1985) commented on these issues from a slightly
different perspective. Attempting to account for a prevalent sense of
frustration and pessimism among social workers, he suggested that
since the Seebohm upheaval in the early 1970s, they were trapped
in an industrial type of line management structure, in which they
were instructed rather than consulted, found themselves embroiled

in a trade-union kind of wrangling, so that their suggestions met with an adversarial response. Woodmansey saw this situation as quite incompatible with the interests of clients, many of whom may be apprehensive, suspicious or aggressive towards someone intervening in their lives, and who need, at the very least, a nonretaliatory response. Even where the problem has a large environmental component requiring practical help, he asserted that interpersonal conflicts and resistance to being helped need to be addressed. The social worker's task of dealing with complex and often self-destructive human functioning can, he suggested, only be achieved with adequate preparation, good supervision and support offered with a minimum of inspecting, judging or inquisitorial pressure. This is, of course, what practitioners of counselling and psychotherapy, and also of social casework in its heyday, have always understood about their own work.

Increasingly in local authorities, the caseload of social workers is not only defined by statute, but is also tending to be restricted to high-priority cases within those groups which in theory have a 'right' to a service. Social workers have to act as rationers and gatekeepers on behalf of society; they have the invidious task of deciding who among the many in need should receive a service, and saying 'no' to the rest. In effect, those referred pass through a series of filters, including eligibility, resource availability, budgetary constraints, and policy guidelines concerning priority. Central government, the local authority or other employer, and the agency team or staff group, all play a part in establishing such filters, but the individual worker bears most of the burden of communicating and implementing them as far as potential clients are concerned. In terms of possibilities for a counselling role in these circumstances, we need to ask how far such a role is hopelessly compromised by these sorts of constraints, and to what extent it is possible to find ways of accommodating them. We then need to identify the precise nature of the practice which emerges, and to examine it in detail in subsequent chapters of this book.

One implication for counselling is the stark contrast that exists between the emotional climate facing a new client of an agency dedicated to counselling and that confronting a new social work client in the busy reception area of a local authority team. We know how difficult the first help-seeking encounter is for anyone, and how complex are the processes of being referred, articulating and agreeing the issues that might be worked on, and beginning to establish trust in both the help-giver and an often quite unfamiliar way of working. If the counsellor or social worker is free to devote untramelled attention to the client from the start, such problems can usually be worked through in an instructive fashion (Jacobs 1988). Consider, however, the extra difficulty when the worker's anxiety, uncertainty and guilt are heightened by questions about statutory authorization to do the work, whether time will be available, and how realistic the expectations of the client or referring agent are. Almost inevitably, both the social worker and the client will perceive the situation not in a totally open-minded way, but through a smokescreen of agency constraints.

Rationing devices apply not only at the point of referral, intake and allocation, but also throughout the client's contact with the agency, in terms of the length of contact (whether it be long- or short-term, intensive or otherwise), the type of work done, and the range of practical resources made available. It is of course a matter of good professional practice that such issues should be regularly kept under review. It is not in anyone's interest that cases should drift on aimlessly, or that valuable resources should be used indiscriminately. One crucial question here is whether cutting back on the time a social worker spends with a client's family is done for good professional reasons or as a matter of expediency. Yet another crucial question concerns the locus of this sort of decision making: how much discretion is available to the individual practitioner in these circumstances?

This question of discretion in the local authority situation has been thoroughly addressed by Bamford (1990), who looked at the impact of managerialism. By this, Bamford meant the organizational imperatives of the employing agency, expressed in their chains of command and procedural guidance, on the personal values of the worker and the way these can find expression. He found that the worker's freedom of manoeuvre is being restricted not only by shortage of resources and defined policies, but also by external agencies, who may have different priorities, and by political pressures.

For a social worker who values the potential of counselling in a particular situation, a further type of constraint is often experienced, that of a tension between the voluntary and statutory aspects of his or her professional response, and indeed between the 'counselling' and 'managerial' aspects of the situation. This tension can work in two directions. In the first, a social worker may be involved at the client's own request, for example where a single parent asks for help in managing the difficult behaviour of her teenage son. Some trust develops, and the mother, son and social worker struggle cooperatively with the issues. If, however, the son then commits an offence, and there is a request for a Social Inquiry

Report, the social worker returns to the family in a different role, one less acceptable to the mother and son. They now may well see the social worker as judging rather than supporting them. Alternatively, the social worker's initial entry to the family could be expressly for the compilation of a report, a step with which the clients must comply. In the process of completing this report, some related or further problems may be identified with which the social worker could offer help, if the family choose to accept it. This is in some respects no easier, as the following example shows.

Case illustration

Mandy, a thirteen-year-old girl, is sexually abused by a group of five slightly older boys while she is working illegally in a mobile shop. Both a social worker and the police become involved following the incident. The parents are of limited intellect and do not seem very concerned, but Mandy herself talks willingly and openly to the social worker. A case conference has to decide whether the girl's name should be put on the Child Protection Register. The social worker wants to continue her work with the family, feeling strongly that counselling with Mandy alongside a supportive contact with her parents will serve to prevent further trouble and aid Mandy's development at a critical early teenage phase. However, the time constraints of the agency during a period of reorganization militate against this plan. A referral could be made to a specialist voluntary agency 'with more time' such as the Brook Advisory Centre, but how will Mandy see the point of such a transfer, with its attendant loss of a known person (i.e. the social worker), and how might her parents then be helped?

The validity of the social worker's assessment in this particular case is amply confirmed in a report of consultation and research in an inner London borough. There the aim was to provide guidelines for preventive policies and practices for girls and young women within the framework of the Children Act 1989. Three of the fifteen practice recommendations in the report are particularly relevant here:

• Wherever possible, the social worker should work with the young women and their families/carers rather than referring this work on to specialist/outside agencies. These agencies should be used where they have a clear brief, and are able to offer something additional to that already available.
• Time must be allocated for social workers to engage and establish a helping relationship with young women on their caseloads.

The most hopeful prognosis will be where this is enabled to happen. (This was the single most important factor in determining outcome.)

- Aftercare needs to be prioritized with this client group who may well remain 'vulnerable' up to 21 or over. This is important in lessening the likelihood of long-term social work involvement in the future (Brown and Pearce 1992).

In reality, there is unfortunately often a very wide gulf between such practice recommendations and what is actually done. This is one commonly encountered way in which the potential of a counselling role for the social worker can be overridden by resource considerations and short-sightedness. Preventive measures, which would be more effective and more economical in the long run, are all too often given low priority in favour of a patching-up response. It is clear from this overview of 'context' that social work is subject to influences and pressures of many different sorts, often acting in conjunction with each other to make a powerful impact on practice. In delineating these, some fundamental questions about role conflicts and value issues have been raised, which are explored in more detail in the next chapter.

· THREE ·

The practice of counselling in social work

The aim of this chapter is to explore issues faced wherever counselling is done, looking at the specific form they take in social work. Four separate but interconnected areas are considered: boundary issues, value issues, issues concerning discrimination, and self-awareness and motivation for helping work.

THE CONCEPT OF BOUNDARY AND ITS APPLICATIONS

This notion of boundary is a most valuable aid to understanding some of the multifarious transactions between people individually, in their families, in groups and organizations. This concept helps us to look at ways of marking off and establishing the identity of something, by differentiating it from other entities and from its surroundings. It is also concerned with setting limits, as we do in everyday life, for example whenever we delineate what is acceptable from what is not. Boundary definition gives enhanced understanding of the types of relationship and interchange that occur between one entity and another. Such processes are clearly involved when it comes to an attempt to define and analyse a complex process like counselling and to distinguish this activity from other related activities. As I have pointed out elsewhere (Brearley 1992), it is more helpful to think in terms of a boundary *region* or area of overlap, rather than merely a boundary *line*. To focus on the latter tends to result in demarcation disputes, whereas to look at the boundary region aids mutual understanding by exploring the common ground and shared territory and concerns between one group or activity and another. In addition, this boundary region is where leadership functions and management are located. Boundary management of whatever sort involves the apparently contradictory tasks of protecting what is inside from too much impingement, and at the same time adapting and responding to the environment. I believe it is appropriate to look at the boundaries of counselling in these terms.

The boundary regions, not only between counselling and social work viewed as separate entities, but also between the counselling and other components of social work, each contain a large number of ambiguous or conflicting elements, all of which raise practical dilemmas. If these can be teased out and analysed, we can perhaps arrive at a deeper understanding of current practice, the reasons for the particular form it takes, and the challenging questions facing those engaged in it.

Who is the client?

A deceptively simple question is whether the primary focus of the helper is on the individual, the family, the couple, a group, the community or on some combination of these. Even in formal specialist counselling practice, where the remit of the agency appears to make this clear, the position is sometimes ambiguous. For example, a marriage counselling service might be expected to see couples, and a student counselling service to see individual students. Yet the marriage counsellor will often be consulted by and work with only one partner, even though the central focus will remain on the couple's relationship rather than on the wider concerns of the individual seen. Likewise, the student counsellor may well work with groups sharing a common problem alongside the one-to-one work. Agency policy, workers' training, resources available and client need are probably the main determinants of the type of practice which emerges. The actual reality is thus very complex and diverse. In social work this complexity is further compounded by the political, legislative and organizational imperatives already highlighted, and by the vast range of potential clients, some with conflicting needs. For example, social workers have to steer a way through conflicts of interest between family members when, as is often the case, the wishes of parents are at odds with the welfare of their children, or a dependent adult requires more care than is available from relatives but refuses to consider any change. Counselling skills of a high order are needed to achieve a satisfactory resolution in such situations.

Time and place issues

An important ingredient in effective helping is the care and attention given to maintaining appropriate boundaries in relation not only to the task, but also to the frequency and duration of sessions and their location. Again this area is much more straightforward for workers in agencies dedicated to counselling than it is for social workers. In the former setting, the worker can, in effect, make an offer to the client in such terms as: 'I suggest that we meet at this same time every week for the next three months. The session will always be in this room, it will last for an hour, and we will not be interrupted.' By arriving punctually and terminating the session on time, and providing a consistent physical space, the counsellor offers a sense of safety and reliability which the client gradually comes to trust and to use in the service of the difficult work being attempted.

The self-same ideals apply to social work, but in that setting they are infinitely more difficult to achieve. The duration of contact, for example, may be prescribed by some external body such as the court, or restricted by budgetary constraints, and it will therefore be less open to negotiation and mutual agreement. Frequency and length of meetings are similarly variable because of the demands, for example, of producing a report for statutory purposes, responding to fluctuations in a client's medical condition, or coping with a crisis. Even the social worker's own best efforts to be punctual and reliably available may be undermined by emergencies, court attendances and so on.

The location of sessions will vary according to the particular task in hand, with meetings taking place in the office interview room, the client's home, the worker's car, a court corridor, a hospital ward, a drop-in centre and any number of other places. As a trainee counsellor (Nicholas 1992) pointed out, work in the (for him) unusual setting of the client's own living environment can raise complicated boundary issues – movement from room to room, disturbance from television and visitors, delay in being let in or entry refused as expressions of ambivalence, and so on – all of which have to be managed at the time and at best used to further the worker's grasp of the problem.

The challenge for a social worker is to minimize the impact of such constraining factors, to screen out distractions as far as possible, and to create a trustworthy climate despite all the impingements. A further challenge is to use the circumstances in a creative way, turning them to good effect. For example, a car journey by its very lack of face-to-face confrontation may provide a setting in which feelings can be unburdened. A journey can also provide an opportunity for adjusting to change, a much-needed transitional space, as demonstrated by Berry (1971) in an account of work with three children who had to leave their long-term foster home following the death of the foster-mother. An interval of three hours between leaving one situation and arriving at the next was spent partly in a cafe and partly in the car. The social worker used these places of transit to help the children to understand a little better what had happened and why they had to make the move, to express their feelings (which emerged in all sorts of disguised and indirect ways, in behaviour as well as words), and then to address their anxieties about what the new place would be like and how they would adjust to it.

LEVELS OF WORK IN THE HELPING PROCESS

Thinking in boundary terms is the approach used by Brown and Pedder (1991), who in turn draw on work by Cawley (1977) in distinguishing different levels of psychotherapeutic communication on a continuum of increasing depth. This continuum ranges from outer levels, in which problems are aired, feelings expressed and support elicited, to the deeper levels of detailed exploration and reexperiencing of past conflicts and relationships as practised in psychoanalysis. The intermediate area, which is dependent on a deepening relationship, includes thorough clarification of problems and confrontation of defences. This sort of thinking helps to clarify the ways in which counselling both differs from and also shares common ground with befriending and psychotherapy, respectively.

Counselling and befriending

A very common first step for most of us when distressed is to seek out a friend in whom we can confide, someone who will listen sympathetically, act as a sounding-board, and give support and encouragement. This informal unburdening or 'getting it off our chest' is a basic ingredient in practically all types of more formal helping relationships. We do not expect that our friends will necessarily have any special training or expertise; all we look for is a degree of trustworthiness and a readiness to spend time trying to tune in to the situation. Such encounters often include an element of confrontation, perhaps in terms of feedback about our own share of responsibility for the problem. They may also, less helpfully, include advice-giving of the 'If I were you . . . !' variety, which we often disregard or follow selectively.

These processes of unburdening, ventilation of feelings and discussion, so familiar in their informal manifestations in everyday life,
are also basic ingredients in practically all types of more formal
helping relationships. However, the very existence of this common
ground can lead to a degree of ambiguity, perhaps best expressed
in the distinction between 'being a professional' and 'behaving professionally'. A vivid example of this is provided in a study of the
work of a telephone helpline (Colman 1989). Such helplines tend
to be staffed predominantly by volunteers, and they exist outside
the professional network of services, offering supplementary or
alternative help to a somewhat different range of users. In this particular case, the service was for parents under stress, especially those
at risk of abusing their children. Volunteers already had access to
professional 'back-ups', mainly social workers, and also to support
groups. They then asked the Institute of Marital Studies to help
them to find ways of coping better with the increasing complexity
of the calls they were receiving, and in response two series of regular workshops, each lasting several months, took place. These helped
participants to improve the quality of their listening and to gain
confidence in setting limits to the most inappropriate calls. In effect,
this made them more 'professional', and yet they wanted to continue as an alternative to the professional services. As one volunteer
said: 'We are *not* counsellors. You have to go from your guts . . . I
don't know how you social workers do it.' She valued the extra
insights gained, but at the same time wanted to preserve the particular informal ethos of the work – a good example of struggling
with boundaries.

In social work, the value of befriending and similar informal
processes of giving and receiving help is so well accepted that many
agencies now try to make provision for its availability to those who
may not always have easy access to friends. Those facing transitions
and crises of various sorts, such as young people leaving care, parents
coping with the birth of a handicapped child, carers of very dependent elderly people, can benefit from informal voluntary help, either
alongside or in place of direct professional input. The social worker's
role in such instances becomes one of catalyst, initiating and enabling
lines of communication, in addition to whatever direct involvement
may be required.

Counselling and psychotherapy

The need for explorations at the margins of each related entity is
well illustrated by perennial discussions about the distinctions and
overlaps between counselling and psychotherapy. There has been a

lot of confusion about this, with much ambiguous writing on the subject. Some authors tend to use the term 'psychotherapy' in such a way as to implicitly encompass counselling, thus denying any difference between the two activities, or at least emphasizing the similarities (Bloch 1982; Kahn and Earle 1982; Dryden 1984; Oatley 1984; France 1988; Hooper and Dryden 1991). Other writers seem at pains to point out the distinguishing features of each, thoroughly teasing out the nature of counselling in its own right as well as its comparisons with psychotherapy, acknowledging the common ground, without denying the complexity of the subject. For example, Worden's (1991) valuable exposition of grief counselling and grief therapy views counselling as facilitating uncomplicated processes, whereas the aim of therapy is seen as being to resolve conflicts of separation which inhibit the healthy completion of mourning tasks. Jacobs (1988) explores the task of assessment for counselling, delineating those factors which indicate the client's potential or otherwise for making use of this approach. Another helpful account of counselling is Noonan's (1983) *Counselling Young People*. Now, despite the fact that the two words are still sometimes used indiscriminately, the literature is becoming much clearer in its acknowledgement of differences as well as common ground between psychotherapy and counselling, and some degree of consensus is beginning to emerge (Jacobs 1988; Dryden *et al.* 1989). It is possible to summarize in tabular form, albeit very crudely indeed, some of the main contrasts which have been identified:

	Counselling	*Psychotherapy*
Location	Wide range of settings	Health care/private practice
Time-scale	Shorter-term	Longer-term
Frequency	Weekly or less	May be more often than weekly
Users	'Clients'	'Patients'
Aim	Strengthen coping abilities	Change determinants of problem
Problem	Recent origin or onset	Longstanding, origin remote
Main focus	External issues	Inner world
Method	Clarification of issues	Work with the transference

In reality, the situation is very much more complex, but it is possible to use such a framework as a rough guide to a continuum of practice. At either end of this continuum, the characteristics of each activity are relatively clear-cut, whereas in the middle ground (or boundary region), where much actual practice is located, there is a great deal of overlap and blurring.

Nearly everyone who comes to see us brings a reality problem to be sorted out and an unconscious to be explored, an anxiety to be relieved and a phantasy to be untangled, an acute need to be helped and a transference relationship to be tested out.

(Noonan 1983: ix)

In general, social work *practice* encompasses the characteristics of counselling rather than those of psychotherapy (using the above crude dichotomies). However, it should be stressed that social work *understanding* can be greatly enhanced by application of insights from psychotherapy and from psychodynamic theorizing. Such applications will be discussed in Chapter Four.

ROLE CONFLICTS IN SOCIAL WORK

I now turn to the consideration of some situations in which the social worker's role as counsellor may have to co-exist with some other role. Here is no simple 'either/or' dichotomy; instead, it is usually a case of 'both/and', in which the social worker has to manage the tensions or contain the paradoxes between apparently contradictory requirements and expectations. As before, thinking in terms of a boundary region can be helpful.

Counselling and/or advice-giving?

Although the public may still associate counselling with advice-giving, – 'We've come so you can tell us what to do!' – most counselling practitioners firmly eschew such a role and regard themselves as essentially or mainly non-directive. Indeed, the demarcation between these two activities is often used to clarify the nature of counselling by including the avoidance of advice-giving in its definition. Agencies have changed their names in order to communicate this point, for example the Scottish Marriage Guidance Council became Marriage Counselling Scotland. The dilemma for social workers is that their role more often than not requires them to offer both advice *and* counselling. This can be confusing for the client. It is also a challenging task for the worker to combine these functions without losing some of the essential elements of counselling.

Direct work and/or environmental treatment?

For those working in agencies entirely dedicated to counselling, the question of engaging in anything other than direct face-to-face work with clients may rarely arise. Expectations and assumptions shared by client, worker and agency are likely to confine the whole encounter to work in the appointed sessions. Modifying the wider situation of the client is generally not seen as the responsibility of the counsellor.

On the other hand, for those who use counselling as just one component of their work, for example in health or educational settings, a different situation pertains, in which much work is done with other people and agencies impinging on the client's life. This is especially true of social work, where a significant proportion of the total time spent on a case may be taken up with indirect contact. Work of this sort has been variously called indirect treatment (Richmond 1917), environmental or milieu work (Hollis 1972), and resource mobilization (Bar-On 1990). One of the pioneering figures of social work, Mary Richmond, first drew this distinction between 'the influence of mind on mind' and the changes brought about by the worker in the client's human and physical environment. Indirect, environmental work then suffered a long period of relative neglect, 'a hidden face of social work practice' as Bar-On (1990) called it, relegated to second-class status and not seen as requiring much skill. It was also wrongly regarded as non-psychological, as if it were not mediated through relationships. Now, perhaps because the impact of environmental deficiencies on people's welfare is more fully acknowledged, indirect work is being given the attention it deserves, and the skills it requires, such as advocacy, bargaining, conflict resolution and negotiation, are being fostered.

Counsellor and/or agent of social control?

As the discussion of the legal framework of social work in Chapter Two indicated, social workers face a particularly acute role conflict whenever they have to involve clients in experiences of compulsion. Much of their work with offenders and with child protection, and all compulsory admissions to hospital or residential care, fall into this category. The Barclay Report referred to it as 'social policing' and considered it essential that social workers should, in strictly defined circumstances, continue this role. Referring to investigation of possible instances of children being harmed by their parents, the Report added:

> We recognise that such investigations, and the surveillance which may follow from them, are disliked by many clients and open to abuse. None the less, we cannot believe they would be better conducted by civil servants or by the police. We also

consider that they require the same skills in planning and
counselling as other tasks performed by social workers.

(Barclay 1982: 47)

Social work is in a unique position here. No other context of
counselling involves the worker in issues of social control and
their accompanying dilemmas to anything like the same degree.

Counsellor and/or social reformer?

A further boundary question, already mentioned in Chapter Two
in relation to the political climate of social work, is the extent to
which the worker has a responsibility to be an agitator, attempting
to change the system. Since the 1970s, social workers have been
unhappy to be seen as simply helping clients to adjust to their
misfortunes, given the gross inequalities of access to health care,
housing, education and employment which undoubtedly exist in
the current social and economic structures. If, as seems evident,
many of the problems faced by clients are rooted in poverty and
disadvantage, then political action may be a more effective remedy
than counselling. On the other hand, some people cope well with
life in precisely the same social circumstances as others who function only with the severest difficulty, and structural explanations
alone cannot explain these discrepancies. A single approach, therefore, whether political action, counselling or anything else, cannot
adequately address the whole situation. Social workers have to be
equally concerned with clients' inner problems *and* with their
environment; furthermore, it is imperative that they work at the
interface of these areas of concern and address the interaction
between them. Jordan similarly argues that, because social workers
are sandwiched between those in political control and the most
powerless, disadvantaged and disaffected groups in society, it is part
of the skill of social work to negotiate with such groups. But, he
says, 'as well as negotiating *with* clients (individually and in their
neighbourhoods, groups and communities) social workers should
also negotiate *on behalf* of clients with their political masters'. He
adds a further role for social workers; trying to encourage client
groups towards fuller, more direct participation in the political process
(Jordan 1984: 121–2).

Assessment: A key to boundary management

The foregoing discussion and illustration of a number of key boundary issues has raised many more questions than it has answered.

How much of the work should be carried out directly with clients and how much with the wider social systems impinging on them? Should the change effort be focused only on the specific individual problem referred, or on bringing about improvements of policy or service for the benefit of a whole range of people facing similar difficulties? How should the balance be struck between work with a vulnerable elderly person and that with the network of carers? Would the setting up of a self-help group for those sharing a common difficulty, such as a disabling illness, be a more effective approach than trying to help just one of them? Might intervention with the family as a whole achieve more than separate work with one or other family member? The answers to questions of this sort are by no means self-evident, and there is always a degree of risk in opting for one course of action and neglecting another. To a much greater extent than others who counsel as part of their job, social workers have to grapple with these dilemmas in almost every situation they handle.

Illustration

The following example shows an organization trying to grapple with some of these dilemmas in its everyday practice.

A voluntary social work organization set up a project to work in the relatively uncharted territory of work with sexually abused young people who themselves were now abusing others. Workers quickly came across some very strong attitudes – of denial, of feeling threatened or judgemental – on the part of both the public and other professionals. Unless they could address these, by enabling their expression and offering more understanding of the problem, their work was in jeopardy through lack of cooperation. Furthermore, as they began to work with the young people in their family context, they commonly found that parents shared their own experiences of having been abused; such material could not be overlooked, but *who* should do the necessary in-depth counselling with these parents? If they took it on themselves, the project workers would have to restrict the numbers of young people seen, a factor on which their future funding depended. Other agencies in the area were extremely hard-pressed and reluctant to take on extra responsibilities. As specialists in a high-risk area of work, they also found themselves very often needing to act as consultants to other workers, for example those in institutions for young offenders, teachers, psychologists or social workers as yet inexperienced in child protection.

What at first sight seemed to involve mainly a specialist counselling role with young people could then be seen as of necessity
requiring them to engage in public relations, consciousness-raising,
educative and consultative work with colleagues, conjoint family
work with parents and teenagers, intensive counselling with adult
victims of abuse, overall case management, and evaluation of the
work to ensure ongoing funding. How should they prioritize these
tasks within the constraints of time, resources and skill? How best
should they cope with the contradictory demands of in-depth direct
work and influencing the environment and climate of opinion?
What actually happened in the second phase of work, following the
realization of the dilemma, was a period of trial and error, of testing
out the boundaries between this agency and others doing related
work, and most importantly, of regular review so that learning
from experience could be used to fine-tune the remit of the agency.
Only then were the workers in a position to give a clearer message
about their function to the outside world, and even this will need
to be adapted periodically.

How do social workers try to resolve such issues as these? Assessment skills of a high order are perhaps the most important requirement of all. Assessment in social work is seen as an ongoing process,
in which the client participates, which explores the interaction
between past events and current circumstances, and which looks at
the strengths and weaknesses of both the people involved and the
available resources. Various theoretical frameworks are used to help
focus on relevant phenomena while screening out those which
may be less pertinent. The challenge of the task is conveyed well
in the following statement:

> The skill of undertaking and producing an assessment depends
> on administrative talent coupled with human relations skills.
> It takes someone who can organise, systematise and rational-
> ise the knowledge gathered together with a gift for sensitivity
> in taking in the uniqueness of each person's situation. 'Hard'
> knowledge such as facts are pertinent, but so too are thoughts
> and feelings and the worker's own clarified intuition.
>
> (Coulshed 1991: 24)

VALUE ISSUES

Social work . . . requires its practitioners to reason with distressed people about the most contentious moral issues in their

society, and to negotiate about the most difficult aspects of human relationships.

(Jordan 1990: v)

This statement provides an explanation for social work's longstanding preoccupation with value questions, principles and ethical dilemmas. The social work literature appears to contain more substantial debate and heart-searching about these areas than does the literature on counselling in general or indeed that of any other professional area concerned with human relations. Whether such social work writing is clear, coherent, readily applicable to actual practice, and relevant to newly emerging problems or political change is quite another matter.

> Asking the question 'What are social work values?' tends to evoke a slightly impatient response. 'Well, they are things like self-determination, acceptance, confidentiality, respect for the individual and so on.' Such a response normally acts as a conversation stopper, but it at least outlines the belief in a clutch of important ideas taken as somehow canonical in the broad church of social work.

(Timms 1989: 14)

Certainly 'respect for persons' has been accorded a central and fundamental place by moral philosophers (e.g. Downie and Telfer 1969), and social work thinking has always endorsed this (Biestek 1961; BASW 1975; CCETSW 1991). A further basic value assumption is the belief in the 'social nature of man as a unique creature depending on other men for the fulfilment of his uniqueness' (Butrym 1976: 45). How might concern for and about the individual be harmonized with such a conviction about the essential interdependence of human beings and their crucial need for relationships? It is the working out of apparent contradictions like this that constitutes the real challenge to practitioners. Butrym adds a third basic value to these; namely, a belief in the human capacity for change, growth and betterment. This of course depends on the extent of freedom of choice possessed by an individual, a much-disputed variable. She argues that these three assumptions 'are in themselves not specific to social work, albeit . . . indispensable to it. They provide a general justification for social workers' involvement in efforts at amelioration of the human predicament' (Butrym 1976: 48).

Instrumental guidelines are then needed, such as Biestek's (1961) formerly well-known 'principles of the casework relationship' – individualization, purposeful expression of feeling, controlled emotional involvement, acceptance, the non-judgemental attitude, client self-determination, confidentiality. It is easy to pay lip-service to vague concepts like self-determination; it is much more difficult to look squarely at the variety of meanings encompassed in the principle, at the ways it may conflict with other deeply held values, such as people's needs for protection or direction, and at the optimum ways of balancing rights and risks. Similarly, as we shall see in the discussion of confidentiality in multidisciplinary and inter-agency work in Chapter Five, the enactment of this principle is a complicated and often perplexing activity, because of obligations which may conflict with or transcend an individual's absolute right to secrecy.

Much of this discussion of values so far could apply with equal force to counselling in other contexts. Both the British Association of Social Workers (BASW) and the British Association for Counselling (BAC) have produced detailed codes of ethics and have continued to debate and amend these in the light of changing circumstances and more consideration (BASW 1975; BAC 1984, 1985; Watson 1985). Further common ground may be seen by comparing the following two statements:

> The values of social work . . . can essentially be expressed as a commitment to social justice and social welfare, to enhancing the quality of life of individuals, families and groups within communities, and to a repudiation of all forms of negative discrimination.
>
> (CCETSW 1991: 15)

The values of counselling have been described as:

> . . . a commitment to encouraging individual and group growth and autonomy within a wider framework; to goal setting and output as well as process; to prioritising and making decisions; to thinking things through and being open; to liberation from oppression and elitism; to supporting and valuing the kind of leadership that facilitates leadership and empowering in others; to cherishing and respecting each other.
>
> (Charles-Edwards 1988: 10)

Given this partial consensus over values, what are the distinctive features of social work's value position, and in particular how do these affect the counselling component of the work? Part of the answer to this is to be found in the societal context of social work. As we saw in Chapter Two, the unique position for social workers is their employment for the most part in large bureaucracies, the fact that much of their activity is determined by statute, and the increasing tendency for their role and functioning to be subject to political debate and scrutiny by the media. As Payne (1985) argues in a critique of the BASW Code of Ethics, because social workers are subject to the authority of their employers rather than directly accountable to clients, there may be a conflict between their responsibility to the agency and their personal professional responsibility to clients. Power is at the root of this ethical dilemma, in that powerful organizations may have interests at variance with the users of their services, and they may wish to promote their own interests to the detriment of those users. Social work managers, as possible signatories of the code of ethics, are especially prone to conflicts of interests and divided loyalties, Payne suggests. This is because of their position as agency representatives coupled with their responsibility for social workers and their concern for the well-being of clients. Bamford echoes and amplifies these ideas:

the growth in managerial power consequent upon the size of social services departments and their bureaucratic structure threatens to subjugate ordinary morality to organizational morality. Social work's contribution to a humanizing influence within the welfare system will itself be threatened if this trend continues. Thinking about values is hard work. Without that thinking, the survival of social work as anything other than a local government function is in peril.

(Bamford 1989: 154)

Empowerment of clients and their participation in decisions and defining services

The BASW Code of Ethics lays on social workers the duty to help their clients both individually and collectively to increase the range of choices open to them and their powers to make decisions. This means enabling clients to identify realistic choices by providing individuals and groups with full information on which decisions can be based, and encouraging self-advocacy. Ideas about a more participatory approach have been debated in social work for many years, but it has taken until quite recently for them to be treated with the seriousness they deserve, and there is still no clear consensus about their implications. However, the climate of opinion is now more favourable than previously to greater involvement of service users, with consumer choice as part of government policy, and the emerging of more groups concerned with the rights of users. Children in care, people with physical disabilities or with learning difficulties, carers and claimants are among those with a much stronger voice than previously. Apart from the fact that this is a democratic activity, and that most people want to have a say in their own affairs, it has been argued that participation can increase the efficiency and cost-effectiveness of services. Certainly it makes for better accountability of organizations, and provides an opportunity to challenge the various forms of discrimination institutionalized in our society. Above all, it is congruent with social work values (Croft and Beresford 1994).

Gender differences in help-seeking

So far, both workers and clients have been referred to generally, without reference to their identity as women or men. Until relatively recently, the significance of gender in counselling and social work was not given the attention it warranted, despite the fact that an eminent American social work writer, Kadushin (1976), had described gender issues as embedded in social work practice and provision. Now there is greater awareness that women and men seek and use personal help in markedly contrasting ways, and equally that each sex is regarded and responded to very differently by agencies and workers. A psychoanalyst, Mike Brearley (no relation!), noticed that, in both marriage counselling and in a psychotherapy unit, the person coming for help was three times more likely to be a woman than a man, and of those taken on for treatment more than 75 per cent were women. If anything, this trend is even stronger in social work. Why should this be the case? The commonly held view is that it is less socially acceptable for men to be depressed or to cry.

> My male patients tend to be cut off from their feelings . . . They experience less conscious misery, or are vaguely miserable but unable to say or know why. By their blank exterior they may cause others also to feel unhappy, or shut out, or hostile. Their experience of their own inner world may also be blank; they cannot remember their past with any vividness, and they avoid strong feelings in the present.
>
> (Brearley 1986: 3)

Brearley goes on to hypothesize that part of the reason may lie in the fact that men are onlookers of pregnancy, birth and child-rearing and somewhat excluded from the emotional and physical changes experienced by their partners. This compounds the dual influence of bodily differences and their psychological impact and the influence of sex roles imposed on children by society, resulting in women being more in touch with their inner life than men.

Such ideas are debated in more depth in a thought-provoking study of tears by Kay Carmichael (1991). She spoke to many people about their experiences of crying and weeping. Men were as eager to talk as women, but nearly all the men feared that they would be laughed at, seen as weak. They envied what they saw as women's greater freedom to express their feelings. One man wrote: 'Men need to re-learn how to cry but first they need to unlearn their coping skills in emotional situations. I learned to hide, to pretend, to disguise my pain and hurt . . . part banter, part clown, part control, part aggression.' If the function of tears is to express some of our deepest feelings – grief, anger, fear, pain, joy – and to signal the need for a response, for attention, then it follows that all of us, boys as well as girls, adults as well as children, will want to cry some-times, and that this is a healthy requirement. Yet the ethos of our society is generally to discourage boys from crying and to react to the tears of an adult with embarrassment. Most boys are encour-aged, by a whole range of subtle processes starting at birth and continuing into adulthood, to be assertive, aggressive and often scornful of their own tender, sensitive or vulnerable aspects. Such powerful socialization must have a great impact on the gender expectations and assumptions with which people, whether workers or clients, approach a counsellor or social worker.

Case illustration: A pilot divorce counselling service for men

Jane Forster, a social worker employed in a voluntary organization concerned with single parents, became interested in the apparent reluctance of separating or divorcing men to seek social work or counselling help, and decided to explore ways of making the help offered more acceptable and useful. She was aware of research findings indicating how devastated men were by the break-up of their marriages, and how several major areas of their lives, namely contact with their children, their health, their work and any sub-sequent partnerships, were likely to suffer for years. She therefore set up a small project to offer both information and counselling to divorcing men. First came a leaflet, 'Alone after Marriage', which explained some of the basic practical issues many men face follow-ing separation, acknowledged the likelihood of experiencing intense emotions, and gave encouragement to readers to 'find someone to talk to'. A small counselling service for men was then offered over the next two years, and the findings from this collated (Forster

1988). One lesson was that it was vital to emphasize and balance two key elements – understanding of feelings (such as depression and loneliness) and specific guidelines. Men came at very different stages of the separation process. Many needed straightforward factual information. Others came when they were on the brink of making an important decision, wishing to clarify their options and prepare a course of action. These were the ones for whom counselling on crisis intervention lines over a period of weeks might have been extremely productive, but it was difficult to engage them in this, as they had not envisaged it and seemed unprepared to allow themselves such an opportunity. The worker came to see the first interview as a challenge to be as effective as possible, partly because it might prove the only opportunity, partly as a way of encouraging further contact – some did indeed later return intermittently. Only a few men came explicitly to unburden and disentangle their feelings; these tended to be seen over a longer period. All needed help to hold on to their sense of identity and self-esteem. An overall impression was not that a men-only service was needed, but that the existing fragmented services needed to be much better coordinated, with the needs of men firmly in mind.

ISSUES CONCERNING DISCRIMINATION

I have already referred to the extent of inequality and oppression in modern British society, and I now look at some of the implications of this in practice. There is accumulating evidence in social work of a much more urgent concern than existed previously both to understand and to try to counteract the problem. Is there a parallel concern in the wider sphere of counselling practice? My impression is that in both fields actual progress is patchy, with some practitioners and agencies making real changes in attitudes and response while others lag far behind. I propose first to spell out the issues as they are being faced up to in social work practice and social work education, including the pitfalls and shortcomings, then to examine the implications of these insights and experience for the counselling component in social work.

The process of official acknowledgment that real problems of prejudice and imbalance of resources exist has not been straightforward even in social work, where evidence for them appears overwhelming. Denial and complacency are still prevalent. The next step, actually addressing the problem, is proving to be extremely complex and not without considerable tension and conflict. That this is so should not be surprising, given the magnitude of change in both attitude and practice which is being attempted, and the amount of vested interests involved. Before looking at attempts to combat racism, some brief definitions are offered.

Racism is defined variously as 'the belief in the inherent superiority of one race over all others and thereby the right to dominance' (Lorde 1984: 115) and as 'a set of economic, political and ideological practices through which a dominant group exercises hegemony over subordinate groups' (Hall 1980: 338). Racism may be individual, institutional and cultural, and these three elements tend to interact and to reinforce each other. This is different from *ethnocentricism*, in which 'the alleged inferiority, disabilities and negative traits of the out groups are thought to be culturally determined whereas in racism there is a belief that the disabilities are inborn . . . but in practice it is not easy to distinguish between racism and ethno-centricism' (*Encyclopaedia Britannica*, quoted by Triseliotis 1993). The term *black* generally refers to '. . . people mainly from South Asian, African and Caribbean backgrounds and other visible minorities in Britain . . . The expression of being Black has not been in contradiction with cultural diversity and ethnic differences. On the contrary, for many minority ethnic people, it has been a source of unified strength and solidarity, opening up more opportunities for celebrating and affirming ethnic identity' (Ahmad 1990).

It might be useful to look at the factors, both driving forces and constraints, which have influenced the establishment of such awareness as exists at present. Official government policy since the early 1960s tended to combine immigration control with various anti-discrimination measures (e.g. the Immigration Acts 1960 and 1971), together with limited amounts of positive policy (e.g. Section 11 of the Local Government Act 1966). The Commission for Racial Equality was set up in 1976. By the 1980s it was clear that legal prescription was having little impact on the fundamental problems of urban poverty compounded by racial issues. These surfaced in riots in Bristol, Brixton and elsewhere, following which the Scarman Report (1981) was published, and at least some local authorities became more conscious of and committed to tackling these problems. Yet at the same time the 1981 Nationality Act tended to support the 'new racism' by providing for repatriation for those denied British citizenship, excluding from nationhood those black British persons whose culture seemed to be seen as inferior to that of the white indigenous population.

Several distinct approaches can be discerned in successive attempts of social work practitioners and educators to address injustice

based on racism (Ahmed *et al.* 1987; Dominelli 1988). First came
the *assimilationist position*, an expectation that black people would
conform with and thereby become more integrated with the (white)
British way of life. This was based on the traditional liberal attitude
that everyone should be treated the same, 'people are people',
regardless of culture or origin – the so-called *colourblind approach*. The
significance of different skin colour is discounted, and other differences such as cultural traditions or varieties of family patterns are
either disregarded or viewed as inferior. When closely examined,
these attitudes can be seen actually to endorse institutional racism
by ignoring the specific strengths and contribution of black people,
viewing them as 'the problem', denying real inequalities, and by
failing to adapt the structure of services and counselling methods
which were originally designed to respond to the needs of the white
community. In social work practice, such an approach would be
expressed in the pattern of employment and involvement of minority people, in neglecting to provide information or interpreters in
minority languages, and in not paying attention and respect to differences in dietary practice, religious observance, skin and hair care
or social customs. Black people's different family structures and
lifestyles, views about women's roles, or methods of child-rearing,
when viewed from a Eurocentric perspective, may be seen as problematic. While problems do exist, these need to be analysed and
interpreted within the cultural context and way of life of black
people, and measures taken to reflect these analyses in services.
Instead, at present, assessments are largely based on what is seen as
appropriate for the white community, and thus resource provision
reflects only the assumptions and requirements of the dominant
group.

An attempt to counteract the worst aspects of such attitudes may
be seen in the next set of ideas to emerge, the *multicultural approach*
coupled with an *ethnically sensitive perspective*, in which cultural diversity is acknowledged and better understanding is sought of the
religions, traditions and customs of specific ethnic minority groups.
Some progress was and is still being achieved by this approach, such
as opening up more dialogue between white and black people,
examining the implications for the helping process when client and
worker are culturally distant from each other, and seriously questioning the use of books and other resource materials dominated
by a white Eurocentric perspective. There may also now be some
correcting of the hitherto serious lack of emphasis, pointed out by
Triseliotis (1986), on the skills, strengths and contribution of people

in minority groups. Despite this progress, however, multicultural approaches, at least in their earlier manifestations, were open to criticism for tending to perpetuate stereotypes of particular cultures, and of their one-sided focus on ethnic minority groups as opposed to looking at white people's use of power imbalances.

A response to this criticism was to use *black perspectives* (Ahmad 1990) more explicitly in attempting to foster *racism awareness*, in effect redefining the problem as in the white population. Courses were provided to raise consciousness in participants of their own personal racism. Some stopped short there, and were criticized for failing to address the structural dimension, and for provoking either a paralysing sense of guilt or a reaction of denial. A way of countering these limitations and problems is embodied in the current prevalence of *anti-racist initiatives*, which aim not merely at understanding racism, but at actively trying to eradicate it.

> Social workers need to be able to work in a society which is multiracial and multicultural. CCETSW will therefore seek to ensure that students are prepared not only for ethnically sensitive practice but also to challenge and confront institutional and other forms of racism . . . also that students are prepared to combat other forms of discrimination based on age, gender, sexual orientation, class, disability, culture, religion, language (including sign language) or nationality.
>
> (CCETSW 1991: 11)

This statement summarizes an important educational and training aim for students undertaking the Diploma in Social Work (DipSW), the professional qualification for social workers and probation officers in whatever setting or sector they work. It exemplifies an anti-racist, anti-discriminatory stance, and shows that oppression and discrimination are concerns which are now being taken extremely seriously by social work educators. It is not yet clear how far this aim is bearing fruit in influencing actual social work practice. The strongest impetus for change seems to have been most evident in the fight against racism, more so than against other forms of discrimination, although work to combat sexism and to address seriously the various manifestations of gender discrimination is gaining ground. It may not be entirely unrealistic to hope that change of heart in one area could bring about change in another; so that a climate of opinion is gradually established in which scrutiny of stigma on the grounds of disability, age or poverty, for example, may perhaps become more likely.

Transcultural work: Practice implications

Because counselling is essentially work about relationships and is mediated through relationships, people's ways of handling encounters with others and the responses they elicit from others are of crucial significance. These issues are addressed in detail by d'Ardenne and Mahtani (1989). Also of particular interest to counsellors is a privately circulated paper about the subtler forms of ethnocentricism and racism by John Triseliotis. He argues that: '. . . expression of emotions and feelings, the display of moods, the tone of voice, physical contact, posture, facial expression and gestures, the management of conflict and the observance of personal and psychical boundaries are all shaped and bound by culture and by cultural norms, rules and experiences. As a result, people from ethnic minority groups who handle their day-to-day interactions in ways that are familiar to them but may not always conform with ethnocentric expectations may be negatively discriminated.'

A process is thus set in train whereby inaccurate assessment on the part of the dominant group leads to critical judgement and derogatory labelling, expressed (especially in middle-class institutions) in subtle and disguised ways. Because the majority cultural group holds the power, ethnic minority people are then likely to suffer actual disadvantage and victimization in the workplace or in access to services and resources.

One fundamental question is whether counselling practice based on Western values is even appropriate at all for some ethnic groups who may not give priority to, for example, individual needs as opposed to those of the family or community.

Illustration: Work with Vietnamese refugees

An informative comment on this issue comes from Bang (1983), who trained Vietnamese and Chinese interpreters as field workers with Vietnamese refugees, and later reviewed with them their experiences of the helping situation and the ways their role developed. Some marked contrasts emerged between their counselling approach and that of their British colleagues. Above all, the Vietnamese fieldworker 'came more as a friend', consciously avoiding being seen as an official or even a professional, taking care to be modest and to show respect, using the proper addressing system, and being prepared to share some personal information. Understanding of cultural norms to do with handling problems underpinned the precise timing and style of approach, as well as its content.

Because it was alien in this culture to let outsiders into one's personal, private sphere, and vitally important that the client should not lose face, problems were approached more indirectly and slowly, not bluntly stating a clear purpose in coming at the outset but waiting to see if the client raised the issue, and then using allegories and parallels gently to gauge the feelings about it. In marital problems, the worker seemed to play the part of advocate or judge, helping the couple to negotiate new rules rather than analyse their conflict. Although psychological pain was shared, there was sensitivity to these clients' fear of focusing on highly emotional areas and putting words to them.

Illustration: Intercultural therapy

NAFSIYAT is one agency which has grappled with the challenge of examining the therapeutic issues which arise whenever worker and client differ in culture, gender, race or socio-economic group. This Intercultural Therapy Centre was set up by Jafar Kareem in 1983 to provide help with mental health problems for people from cultural and ethnic minorities, whose needs are not generally well-served because of the ethnocentric bias of existing services. NAFSIYAT also aims to raise awareness and promote open debate among practitioners. It is based on the conviction that the whole being of the patient has to be taken into account, including any real-life experience of racism, and that the assumptions of both patient and therapist about, say, family relationships, have to be addressed from the start (Kareem 1978).

These examples of practice in specific agencies raise many questions for Western workers who in order to work effectively across cultural boundaries will have to examine deeply held and usually implicit aspects of their own beliefs and values.

What other conclusions can be drawn from this sampling of trends, experiences and ideas related to anti-discriminatory practice? First, it is clear that any single strand of endeavour on its own will not be able to achieve significant and lasting progress. It is not sufficient to enhance understanding of other cultures without at the same time becoming aware of the extent of oppression based on individual and institutional racism. It is not enough to be aware of such injustice without taking active steps to combat it through anti-racist practice. Counteracting racial discrimination and prejudice requires that similar attention and effort be given to gender issues and sexism, and to all the other 'isms'. It is vital that those concerned with education and training for social work or counselling practice cooperate closely with practitioners and agencies, as progress in one sphere can easily be blocked by resistance, ignorance or apathy in the other.

This is a field where counselling in general has much to learn from CCETSW initiatives in social work education, from both the achievements and the problems experienced. What CCETSW (1991) has attempted is to spell out and monitor specific requirements for anti-discrimination in the knowledge, values, skills and competence of qualifying social workers, and then also to provide detailed guidance in how to achieve it (e.g. Phillipson 1992; Humphries *et al.* 1993).

Most recent social work texts (e.g. Bamford 1990; Jordan 1990; Preston-Shoot and Agass 1990; Clarke 1993) include much debate about inequality, racism or sexism, whereas some recent counselling literature contains none (e.g. Dryden and Thorne 1991; Corney and Jenkins 1993; Howe 1993). An important insight from work done already is that this is not a separate subject to be dealt with in isolation, but rather has to permeate and inform all aspects of the work – practice, education and training, and the literature.

SELF-AWARENESS AND MOTIVATION FOR HELPING WORK

What makes people first become interested in counselling or social work? What sorts of interests, experiences and needs prove influential as this interest develops? These deceptively simple questions could be answered by each person at a lot of different levels, some quite obvious, some more complicated, and others of which one may be only dimly aware, reflecting hidden bits of experience and personality:

- A friend told me about it. I was looking for a new challenge.
- My religious (or political) belief was the motivating factor.
- We have experienced that problem in my own family.
- I needed help myself once, and it made all the difference.
- I find people endlessly fascinating; I'm curious about what makes them tick.
- I think I'm searching for an answer to my own uncertainties.
- I've always needed to look after people; I like to be the strong one.
- Maybe its something in me that I'm really dealing with when I try to help someone else?

These responses clearly range from altruistic motives through those based on adult life experience to underlying expressions of need arising much earlier on, and different influences probably co-exist within any given individual. The most powerful ones are likely to be those of which there is the least awareness.

Self-questioning is therefore a vital ingredient in a good counsellor's approach, not only in teasing out factors in the choice of such work, but also, and especially, the ways in which the work is conducted. Unless increasing self-awareness can be developed, there will be a real danger of workers using clients to meet their own needs, and of the workers' blind spots denying them the help they require. All this is, of course, a life-time's struggle, not just a matter of initial motivation. Unless the worker knows what he or she brings into the situation, how can the precise nature of what the client brings be properly assessed? What is needed is for the worker to become a well-regulated barometer of all the feelings in the encounter, able to sort out which feelings belong to whom.

Self-gratification and exploitation of clients are rarely discussed in the helping professions. Exploration of underlying motivations brought to the work tend to lead to some uncomfortable questions. What is the role of altruism? In what particular ways might the impingement of workers' own needs be detrimental for service-users? Such issues are addressed in a thought-provoking and helpful paper, 'Make sure to feed the goose that lays the golden eggs' (Skynner 1989). Skynner's discussion focuses on social workers, but it has equal relevance for all those engaged in counselling. Those who enter the helping professions to perform a difficult and thankless task ('the geese') may be willing to do so because they can thereby satisfy their own psychological needs. Many sneak into caring agencies by the staff door to get help for themselves without acknowledging their own need, Skynner suggests. The agency serves as an arena where important aspects of the worker's childhood can be relived and personal needs expressed in behaviour if not always in words. Avoidance of exploitation of clients can only happen if workers can experience their own real needs directly (rather than vicariously through clients), and can be offered appropriate satisfaction of them ('the feeding') by means of adequate personal and professional development. How can this be achieved? Ideally, a combination of good supervision, case discussion groups, continuing in-service training, and effective workload management together provide opportunities to look at the interfaces of self, role and client need. Given such conditions, 'the vicious cycle of (workers') deprivation becomes a virtuous circle of mutual nurture'.

How to find the right balance between *involvement and detachment* is another central issue for social workers and indeed for all counsellors. How close should the practitioner get to the client? How much objectivity is needed? There is a very important boundary issue here, and also a real paradox, because it seems necessary to adopt two opposite positions at once! That is to say, the worker should be prepared to identify with the client and to become emotionally immersed in the situation, and yet simultaneously it is vital to observe and intellectually monitor what is going on. This requires a sort of 'binocular vision'. Of course, it is highly unlikely that the right balance will be achieved all the time. It is more probable that the worker will swing like a pendulum, at some times being swamped in the problem, and at other times being unable to face the cost of involvement and becoming rather too distant or mechanical. This raises again the crucial need for growing self-awareness. It is where a sounding board, a really good supervisor or supportive peer group, can make all the difference.

There is one more reason why development of self-awareness is a vital requirement. Counsellors are exposed to all sorts of primitive feelings and disturbed behaviour. There may be violence, or delinquency, or elements of madness. People whose inner states of mind are chaotic tend to express this in appalling relationships with other people, and by definition they are disturbing as well as disturbed. So those working intensively with them can easily become affected, caught up, and even pushed to retaliate, because such primitive functioning in others is liable to evoke one's own most primitive and unresolved feelings.

It is irresponsible to try to practise in a counselling role in any setting without thorough training and ongoing supervision. These issues will therefore be taken up in the next chapter.

· FOUR ·

Specific issues in counselling in social work

This chapter explores some issues which are of great concern in social work, first by describing them by focusing on their particular implications for the counselling component of social work, and then by identifying points of interest or significance and potential lessons for the wider sphere of counselling.

The intention here is to look at the qualities, skills and knowledge required for competent practice. This includes criteria for selection of social workers, and the training available to them at different stages and levels, including the theoretical input offered and the methods used to impart skills, with particular reference to material concerned with the counselling dimensions of social work. How does selection and training for social work compare with that for counsellors in other fields?

SELECTION

There exists a good deal of consensus about the personal qualities thought to be required of those aiming to work intensively with vulnerable people. Most social work educators would agree whole-heartedly with the need to look at selection for evidence of the following attributes (or of the potential for developing them); this list derives from the British Association for Counselling's counsellor training-course recognition proposals:

- self-awareness, maturity and stability;
- the ability to make use of and reflect upon life experience;
- the capacity to cope with the emotional and intellectual demands of the course;

- the ability to form a helping relationship;
- the ability to be self-critical.

(Charles-Edwards *et al.* 1989: 420)

Most selection procedures, whether for social work or other counselling arenas, use a combination of selection tools – application forms, references, personal statements of motivation and experience, information-giving sessions, individual interviews and group discussions or exercises. Some use is occasionally made of intelligence or aptitude tests. The hope is that qualities or problematic aspects overlooked by one approach may emerge through another; there is an inevitable degree of subjectivity in assessing the sorts of qualities needed, so cross-checking between different interviewers is the norm. Coverage of the applicant's grasp of the reality of the job, its breadth, the stress and type of conflicts involved, and the nature of supervision already experienced is vital whatever the field of work, as is an attempt to ensure that the student will be able to learn in groups of various sizes, and will be open to a range of new ideas. An over-dogmatic attitude and evidence of strong prejudices is clear cause for rejection. Equally, a lack of awareness and concern about value issues would be very worrying.

Social work and counselling courses may differ in the degree of emphasis given to particular criteria, and in the precise selection procedures used to ensure these and other qualities in successful applicants. Another difference may be found in the age and experience of applicants. Many entrants to social work courses are in their middle twenties, some still completing their education and embarking on their first career, perhaps with experience as volunteers or as assistants in social care. Others may have held quite responsible social work posts, possibly in residential work, for three or four years. Some will have much more life experience, perhaps returning to work after a break or making a career change, but unless the course is employment-based, or geared specifically to such entrants, they may be in a minority. By contrast, any substantial counselling course will tend to attract mature students, those already established in a caring job, who wish to deepen or extend their existing understanding of relationship work; some courses do not consider those aged under about thirty. Thus the evidence on which a judgement can be made will vary.

A significant difference may lie in the emphasis placed upon academic achievement and potential. All social work courses, but only some counselling courses, are located in academic institutions, and would-be students have to satisfy their entry requirements. For social work these may range from two 'A' levels (or their near-equivalent for an older student) to a good honours degree. The priority given to academic credentials by trainers of counsellors varies greatly; some regard personal suitability and experience as paramount, and would not see intellectual development as a primary consideration, whereas a university course at masters level would explore conceptual ability and even research potential.

The vital need in helping work for well-developed self-awareness was discussed at the end of Chapter Three. The question now arises, how is its presence ascertained and fostered? It is generally agreed that experience of personal therapy or membership of a therapeutic group are among the best means to develop self-knowledge. For this reason, some counselling courses ask their students to have undertaken some personal work or to be prepared to do so; this is very rarely the case in social work. Whether or not the training body requests or recommends such a step, some applicants may already have been in a client role themselves, and others are likely to seek counselling during the course if the disturbing material they encounter in those seeking their help resonates with something similar in their own background. Having had some traumatic experience, and having gone some of the way towards resolving or accommodating it, is usually seen as giving the potential helper more sensitivity to others in distress; the reverse is true if the experience is still very raw or has had to be denied or otherwise blocked off – in such cases, the potential helper may experience particular difficulties of understanding or over-identification.

These comparisons raise some interesting questions. Should counselling selection include more rigorous scrutiny of intellectual potential? Does the selection process for social work run the risk of underestimating both the need for self-awareness in its practitioners and the personal impact of the work on them? Are social work educators in fact selecting students for their counselling potential in addition to other required qualities? Since it is probable that priorities at the selection stage accurately reflect those within the training itself, then similar questions will need to be asked about course content and approach before conclusions can be drawn.

QUALIFYING EDUCATION AND TRAINING FOR SOCIAL WORK

Early developments

Social work *training* can be properly understood only in the context of the historical background of social work *practice*, which was discussed in Chapter One. Prior to 1950, modern social work education had hardly started. What did exist mirrored precisely the fragmented nature of practice itself, which comprised separate unrelated services, staffed for the most part by people with little or no training. Some in child care and in moral welfare had access to training, and there were *ad hoc* specialized courses for home teachers of the blind and for NSPCC inspectors. A number of universities offered social science courses at the time, well-regarded as offering preparation for social work practice. However, only a tiny minority of social workers were fully trained and they were located almost exclusively in hospitals or clinics and the courts, that is to say, those settings associated with the established professions of medicine and law. This minority – as almoners and psychiatric social workers, together with some probation officers – had already set up professional associations which worked to develop patterns of education and training and also to ensure recognition of their qualifications. These pioneers attained remarkable standards of excellence in casework, that is to say, in practice equivalent in most respects to counselling as we know it today, and in developing working partnerships with other professions. They also exercised considerable influence on wider policy, legislation and professional development. However, their actual numbers were very small indeed. To give an idea of the scale involved, in the 1950s around 90 almoners/medical social workers per year were emerging from courses; even by 1969 there were still only 1100 psychiatric social workers in active employment in Britain (Younghusband 1978).

What happened to change this state of affairs can only be understood by looking at a complex interplay of factors. For example, the cumulative effect of events following the creation of the local authority Children's Departments in 1948 not only led to greatly increased demand for specific professional expertise, and hence for expansion of training opportunities, but it also established a trend which was to continue for the next twenty-five years, namely for social work to be increasingly located within the statutory framework and administrative structure of central and local government. The social climate around the 1960s was conducive to the growth of social work; it was a time when state intervention was seen as the way to tackle the problems of society. Taken together, these processes gave rise to a new type of professionalism – 'bureaucratic professionalism' – mutually beneficial to the state, which needed the services, and to the members of the occupational groups, who needed the organizational base, job security and status. A by-product was the way in which more men entered a hitherto mainly female occupation, attracted by the increased number of managerial posts

(Langan 1993). Social services expanded rapidly, and social work as a profession had to develop to meet the demand.

The stage was thus set for major change and development of social work training opportunities. One change arose from a review of the university social science courses: Did they serve as an adequate training in their own right, or should they more properly be regarded as *pre-professional*, a foundation for full vocational training? When the latter view held sway, not without a great deal of conflict, the impetus was thereby increased to develop more university professional courses to provide a full qualification to some of those with this pre-professional grounding after a further year's study. Another shift was to reduce the hitherto narrow specialist focus of existing casework courses by introducing, experimentally at first in 1954, a new type of education in 'applied social studies' in some universities. This was based on the belief that all social workers require the same basic understanding of human beings and skills in relating to them, and that such learning can be adapted to meet the needs of particular client groups in specific settings. Other aims were to promote better communication among students preparing for work in different types of agencies, to give them an enriched learning experience, and to make better use of limited teaching resources. At that time, the main emphasis remained on in-depth relationship work with individuals and families.

Of immense significance was the fact that these vocational courses were not intended to impart mere technical *training*, but rather to offer a professional *education*, based on academic study of sociology, psychology, social philosophy and social administration, and including the application of concepts and principles to social work practice. This distinctive emphasis on education *and* training, as opposed to just training *per se*, has remained an important and controversial theme in social work to this day, and it has equal relevance for thinking about the most appropriate forms of preparation for counselling. Some critics have argued that in both fields – social work and counselling – the pendulum has swung much too far in the opposite direction, to the extent that we now see training syllabuses which downgrade the dimensions of values and knowledge and focus almost exclusively on technical skills. An unfortunate consequence – and perhaps also cause – of this is the way some social services employers tend to devalue 'critical practitioners' and expect their staff to implement agency policy in an unquestioning way.

A mixture of courses at different levels and with different emphases was beginning to evolve. This partly reflected an ongoing struggle to define more precisely the various facets of the social work

task, based on perceptions of types of client need. An early and very
influential attempt to do this was the Younghusband Report (1959),
which looked into 'the proper field of work and the recruitment
and training of social workers at all levels in the local authorities'
health and welfare services'. The report distinguished three categories of need for social work in these services:

a) People with straightforward or obvious needs who require
   material help, some simple service or a periodic visit who
   could be catered for by 'welfare assistants' with in-service
   training and supervision.
b) People with more complex problems who require systematic help from trained social workers. A new two-year college training leading to a Certificate in Social Work was
   recommended in response to this need. From 1961 these
   courses co-existed with the university routes, but rather
   than expecting a student to gain a theoretical grasp of social
   sciences before moving to a professional course, they
   integrated theory and experience in order to enhance the
   relevance and applicability of the learning for actual practice. This development also set a pattern of dual entry at
   graduate and non-graduate levels which continues to the
   present day.
c) People with problems of special difficulty requiring skilled
   help by professionally trained and experienced social workers. The counselling dimension was assumed to have a high
   profile in this category of need, training for which already
   existed in the universities.

However, the apparently clear distinctions in the degree of challenge and complexity of task which this framework offered proved
to be too difficult to discern in practice, particularly at the point
when a client or family first sought help or came to the notice of
the services. Problems which seem straightforward at first sight often
turn out later to have hidden dimensions, but changing workers
is not generally feasible – an issue which is as alive now, in both
counselling and social work, as ever in the past. Partly because of
this, and also because of the chronic shortage of staff, the clear task
and status differentials envisaged in the Younghusband Report faded.

1970–85

The number and variety of courses increased very significantly, to
the extent that in 1975 ten times as many students were qualifying

as in 1950. The old specialist emphasis was disappearing, and practically all courses were now in varying degrees 'generic', that is to say, imparting to students the principles and skills common to all forms of social work with individuals and families. This shift of emphasis had been accelerated by the recommendations of the Seebohm Report (1968), discussed in Chapter One, which led to the establishment of unified local authority departments drawing together the functions of the previously diverse welfare services. It made sense that social work training should reflect this unifying trend, especially as the report had criticized the separate specialist trainings as educationally and professionally unsound.

Accordingly, in 1971 the Central Council of Education and Training in Social Work (CCETSW) was set up. Its remit was to promote education and training, to recognize courses and to award qualifications, to recruit students and to engage in research in social work education. It covered all fields of social work, including residential care and work in the voluntary sector. It immediately brought into being a new award, the Certificate of Qualification in Social Work (CQSW), for all students who successfully completed recognized courses. The recognition process embarked on by the council at the same time had the effect of harmonizing to a great extent the requirements of the 150 different qualifying courses then in existence and laying a foundation for future developments.

CCETSW's next step, which was both controversial and influential, was to introduce an entirely new form of training to run in parallel with the CQSW. This was the Certificate in Social Service (CSS), originally intended for those working in the social services but not in posts defined as requiring a social work qualification. This training was employment-based as opposed to college-based, less academic and more practical. It was for those already employed, with employers fully involved in the planning and provision of learning. This pattern of training was not intended to be at a lower level – it was supposed to be 'equal but different' – but it nevertheless tended to be seen as having inferior status at first. There was considerable confusion when it came to deciding which staff should undertake CSS as opposed to CQSW. Was the residential care of adolescents not to be defined as social work? Did managers of day care provision not need a sound grasp of social work? Inconsistent reactions to issues like this meant that some senior people in such fields of work did take the CSS. Then, by demonstrating to managers and others the practical value of the learning it offered, these CSS holders gradually but completely transformed the original (inferior) perception of it and undermined the previous elitism.

Over the years the award commanded respect, and achieved – albeit almost by inadvertence as Bamford (1990) suggests – absolute parity with CQSW. The CSS subsequently became to some extent a model for patterns of training which evolved later.

It still proved well-nigh impossible to achieve a consensus as to which tasks warranted a *social work* qualification and which did not, although further attempts were made to do so. The Birch Report (1976), in attempting to delineate those roles which should be performed only by CQSW holders, cited circumstances involving the client in loss of liberty or change of home, whether compulsory or voluntary, and situations needing complex assessment, treatment or planning. Fierce arguments ensued, which were intensified by another stab at the same task by the professional association, which identified three criteria for requiring the intervention of a qualified social worker: (1) level of client vulnerability, (2) degree of case complexity and (3) significance of decision-making (BASW 1977). Just as in the earlier response to the Younghusband Report, practitioners were not at all convinced by the apparent logic of such statements, finding them unworkable in the real world where many unqualified colleagues were undertaking work of this sort.

These developments in the education and training of social workers had been initiated during a phase of growth and hope. Their implementation, however, coincided with a period of increasing stringency and doubt.

> Seebohm was a false dawn for social work. The new era of social service expansion and professional advance for social work turned out to be short-lived. Scarcely had the unifying dynamic of the 1960s ushered in the generic social worker and the social services department, than the forces of fragmentation were unleashed by the combination of economic recession and political retrenchment in the 1970s. In retrospect, Seebohm marked the high tide of social work, the peak of a wave of political and professional optimism that slowly ebbed away over the next decade.
>
> (Langan 1993: 48)

It was during the 1970s that reactions against the predominantly casework/counselling emphasis in many courses began to hold sway. These came from a variety of sources. Other methods of social work, such as group work, community work, and work in residential and day care settings, were claiming more attention, with the result that the knowledge and skills they required were given time in the curriculum previously occupied by casework. At the same time, radical thinkers within social work (Bailey and Brake 1975; Corrigan and Leonard 1978), coupled with vocal groups of clients, started to attack what they perceived to be paternalistic attitudes in the profession and the tendency to explain social problems in terms of individual inadequacy or pathology. They also criticized the prevalent lack of self-criticism and awareness among social workers of the implications of being state employees. A further factor in the reaction against casework could be discerned in changes in the courses' theoretical input. The most influential social work writers in the 1950s and 1960s had been Perlman (1957) and Hollis (1964), whose books could in many respects still serve today as useful manuals of counselling practice. During the 1970s, a different way of thinking, the 'unitary approach' (Goldstein 1973; Pincus and Minahan 1973; Specht and Vickery 1977), was given a more central place in the curriculum. This approach used systems thinking (discussed in Chapter Two), moved beyond the usual focus on the individual client to encompass influences from the wider environment, and offered a more integrated, coherent way of tackling the complex phenomena which underpin assessment in social work. These various interacting trends and pressures had a powerful impact, reducing considerably the pre-eminence of casework or counselling thinking.

It was therefore in a very different climate of opinion and resource provision, both nationally and within social work itself, that in 1982 the Barclay Committee tried yet again to work out a clear formula for differentiating social work tasks. Part of their concern was to ensure that scarce resources were allocated as appropriately as possible, by targetting those most in need and by avoiding the use of highly trained workers for tasks which did not need their expertise – a concern which has a powerful contemporary resonance. Among examples of priority social work tasks identified in the report were the following:

- making a full assessment of need.
- situations where life or liberty are at risk.
- counselling help to enable elderly people and others reach a decision about alternative living arrangements.
- counselling when private sorrows or relationship problems are escalating into life crisis proportions.
- where the client, family or group seems unable to make use of available resources.
- where a network of resources needs to be established and monitored.

(Barclay 1982: 47)

Counselling clearly has a high profile here. The report addressed the criticism that social work training has concentrated too exclusively upon 'direct counselling-type support work with individuals and groups' (Barclay 1982: 44) by recommending that courses should encompass social care planning as well as counselling, without detracting from the latter.

Current qualifying education and training for social work

What happened next, in the mid-1980s, is a further example of the way social work training developments tend to be a product of a combination of professional considerations, media pressure, political expediency and financial stringency. As we saw in Chapter Two, concern about child abuse can act as a strong driving force in public and parliamentary calls for change. In this instance, the pressure was for social work training to be extended from two to three years, an extension which the courses, professional associations and CCETSW all agreed was vital. The existing qualifications had not been able to offer adequate preparation for practitioners struggling to respond to vastly increased and changing demands brought about by legislative and social change, including new ideas about community care, growing awareness of the extent of child abuse, and emerging problems like AIDS. It should be noted that the changing task definitions brought about by these new needs all require extra knowledge and skill, together with a re-working of existing areas of competence. Paradoxically, an even greater need for counselling abilities was emerging in social work at precisely the time when other types of work were claiming more attention. The CCETSW therefore proposed a new three-year award, the Qualifying Diploma in Social Work (QDSW), which would have come into being in 1991, yet despite the undoubted need for longer training the government rejected this. Instead of the £40 million the changes would have cost, a fraction of this was offered for developmental work within the constraints of a two-year programme. In order not to lose momentum and the value of the careful thinking already done, CCETSW agreed to introduce a new two-year award, the Diploma in Social Work (DipSW) to be phased in by 1993–94.

The Diploma in Social Work (DipSW)

What therefore is involved in the DipSW? For professional qualification in social work across the whole range of settings and sectors, it prescribes standards of competence to be demonstrated by students on course completion. Study and supervised practice is to be undertaken at higher education level in programmes provided collaboratively by universities, polytechnics or colleges with social work agencies. All students share a common base of values, knowledge and skills, complemented by a substantial amount of learning in a 'particular area of practice'. Most importantly, they have to show that they can transfer their understanding to new situations. Assessment procedures are carefully regulated. There had always been a wide range of social work courses with many variations in style and emphasis as well as in placement patterns. In focusing on *outcomes* of social work training in the DipSW, CCETSW deliberately chose not to present a particular model, and hoped to maintain and encourage this flexibility and variety in approach. Within the overall framework, and subject to approval (the criteria are quite daunting!), programme providers may structure their input as they see fit. For example, college-based, employment-based and part-time routes to qualification have existed for some time; modular and distance-learning programmes are now being developed.

It was difficult at first for social work educators to avoid a resentful sense of being expected to make bricks without straw, especially since public criticism of social work continued unabated. It was equally difficult for them to cope with yet another period of great turbulence and to make the very considerable adjustments in curriculum design and working relationships necessary to meet the new expectations. As if to add insult to injury, a 'trial by media' of the new DipSW requirements was set in train during the summer of 1993. This was seemingly sparked off by controversy surrounding a well-publicized mixed-race adoption case in Norfolk, in which serious criticism of the work was justified. However, what followed was a welter of more generalized and damaging attacks on CCETSW's concern to equip social workers with an understanding of racism and other forms of discrimination. These were led by Melanie Phillips in the *Observer* (1 August 1993) and by Brian Appleyard in the *Independent* (4 August 1993) and they gave rise to a great deal of editorial comment and correspondence. What was striking was the vehemence of feeling against a form of training that had hardly started – the first few to qualify did not emerge until 1992 and most of the earliest cohorts only completed their courses in 1994 or later. Clearly, any attempt to evaluate a training before its products have had an opportunity to practise is bound to be spurious. Ironically, this was taking place against a background of acknowledgement that the two-year programme was inadequate but that nevertheless there were insufficient resources to extend it. Despite this, the DipSW is to be fully reviewed during 1994, 'to take account of changes in legislation and service needs', with the added urgency imposed by government (CCETSW 1993). Such decisions serve to underline the extreme pressure on social work educators and the massive difficulty of their task.

There are, however, signs that as the dust in some parts of the arena settles, benefits are being experienced from the upheaval; in particular, the much greater degree of local collaboration and partnership in training provision, the more explicit monitoring of standards, the bringing of anti-discriminatory practice into sharper focus, and the significant improvements in the quality of practice placements. This last area of practice teaching and learning is so fundamental to social work education, and indeed to all forms of counselling, that it requires full attention in its own right.

PRACTICE TEACHING IN SOCIAL WORK EDUCATION

Carefully supervised practice has been a central feature of the process of equipping social workers for their role since the start of training in the early decades of the twentieth century, although both the understanding of exactly what it entails and also the extent and quality of provision has varied immensely over the years. At first it was simply seen as spending prescribed periods of time under the direction of an experienced worker, with the emphasis on apprenticeship. Gradually, the educational significance of these placements was acknowledged by utilizing designated 'student supervisors' based in each agency used by the course, to provide live practice situations to which the student could apply theoretical knowledge and other classroom learning, and to offer periodic assessment of the student's progress and performance. From the mid-1950s, there was a spate of writing about supervision on both sides of the Atlantic (Garrett 1954; Towle 1954; Deed 1962; Heywood 1964; Young 1967). The assumptions then prevalent about the nature of the task are very different from those of today. The relationship between teacher and learner was seen as hierarchical, all students were presumed to learn in the same way, to start as naive, empty vessels, and to progress through similar stages. The emotional growth of students was given a lot of emphasis (the work was mainly what would nowadays be called counselling) and this led to blurred boundaries between supervision as an educational process on the one hand, and as a therapeutic process on the other

(Gardiner 1989). Gradually, and especially since the early 1980s, new approaches and attitudes towards practice learning in social work have begun to hold sway.

The findings of one informative research study (Secker 1993) are likely to be of interest to those concerned with the development of competence in counselling in whatever context, not only in social work. In this study, the approaches of student social workers to their practice were explored by means of in-depth interviews focusing on students' recent work in one particular situation. The research had two main aims: to contribute to the development of evaluative methods in social work education, and to understand the influence of different educational activities – the use of theory, the value of various academic teaching approaches, and the significance of placement experiences – on the development of students' practice. The researcher was able to develop a typology of three approaches to practice, distinguished by the sort of knowledge drawn on by students and the ways they used this knowledge. The 'everyday social approach' involved the use of knowledge from personal life rather than any theoretical material. In the 'fragmented' approach, students did draw on theory but experienced problems in linking material from different sources, relating it to their existing everyday knowledge, and using it. The 'fluent' approach was marked by students' capacity to be selective rather than indiscriminate in their use of knowledge handed on to them, and to be able to construct their own 'custom-made' theories to make sense of and guide their response to the situations they encountered. As students progressed through training, this fluent, more integrated approach tended to be increasingly in evidence, although there are dangers in both stereotyping these approaches and over-simplifying the processes of learning.

During the 1980s, concerns about both the quality and quantity of practice learning opportunities were being voiced by many from academic institutions and agencies involved in social work qualifying courses. Therefore, in 1989, CCETSW approved a strategy for tackling these concerns, by introducing new systems of funding provision, promoting better local systems for arranging placements, raising awareness among employers of the importance of high-quality placements, introducing a new system of training, assessing and accrediting practice teachers and approving agencies providing effective practice learning. Such measures built on the good practice which already existed in some areas, but aimed to make it less patchy and more systematic. It is these developments in practice teacher training and accreditation, and the associated debates about how people learn best in practice, which probably have some insights to offer those in other counselling contexts. For example, should not teachers and supervisors in counselling also undertake similar focused preparation and accreditation in practice teaching?

To be eligible for the CCETSW Practice Teaching Award, candidates have to be qualified and experienced social workers who have undertaken at least 150 hours of education and training for practice teaching (in addition to time spent supervising students), and who can demonstrate their ability in no less than fourteen different skill areas, practically all of which are equally relevant to counselling training. The following are examples:

- identify, develop and provide learning opportunities;
- help students to relate theory and practice;
- help students to transfer learning from one situation or setting to another;
- help students to learn the importance of agency policies and procedures;
- draw up a work contract with a student on the basis of his or her learning needs and the requirements of the programme;
- supervise the student's practice as an accountable member of the agency's staff;
- liaise effectively between the college and agency, and within the agency;
- take primary responsibility for the formal assessment of a student's practical and written work while on placement.

Illustration: A supervision session

How does this actually look in practice? Here is part of an account of an actual supervision session, seen through the eyes of an observer (a trainer providing assessment evidence for the award described above). The student was a mature and articulate man on a university postgraduate course nearing the end of his first placement in a voluntary agency concerned with children and families. The practice teacher, P, was particularly able and highly respected by her colleagues.

There was an easy relaxed atmosphere and purposeful attention to the task in hand. The settling period at the beginning included negotiation about the work to be covered. The student was an active participant in this. Part of his agenda was an examination of his own practice, dilemmas and questions in relation to child protection and a particular concern about the possibility of non-accidental injury, to which the student wanted to give thorough consideration. Through constructive feedback, P encouraged a thoughtful and responsible approach. She used the skills of exploration and summarizing to give width and depth to the context and the issues. She explored what had happened and what might have happened, accompanied by positive reinforcement of the student's practice. There was good support to the student over his care and evaluation of the incident, and his management of his own anxiety was commended. The session was consistently student-centred. Examination of theoretical perspectives always arose from the student's material. P's inputs and use of theory and knowledge followed within the student's frame of reference; for example, his statements about a child's need for praise and recognition developed into a fuller discussion of the work of Kellmer Pringle and some research information from the US Headstart Programme. The termination of work commitments as the placement neared completion was covered, leading to an exploration of the developmental stages of children, issues relating to separation and a child's perception of time. The student's own feelings about leaving the placement were acknowledged, and the discussion widened to a consideration of coping mechanisms. The importance of agency policies and procedures was thoroughly handled in relation to child protection. The need for accountability and clear lines of communication was emphasized alongside the desirability of carefully separating issues and possibilities from more concrete and factual material. The student was very eager to learn, and a relationship existed which enabled him to ask for critical feedback and to respond to support and challenge. Progress and overall development were noted, as was the extent to which the student had moved forward in particular areas. A consistent process could be identified whereby questions were raised, dilemmas and doubts explored, followed by investigation of ideas, theoretical perspectives and clues leading to assessment, reassessment and reflection.

'Helpful' and 'unhelpful' practice teaching

This account exemplifies a style of practice teaching highlighted in Secker's (1993) research as 'helpful', an approach in which a supervisor, with warmth, genuine interest and openness to new ideas, places emphasis on identifying and addressing students' learning needs, builds on existing strengths brought to the work, and provides a clear focus on specifics. Its advantages can be seen most vividly when set in juxtaposition with a range of approaches experienced by students as unhelpful, and labelled in some earlier research as 'objectionable' (Rosenblatt and Mayer 1975). Four main types could be discerned. In the so-called 'therapeutic approach', students' problems in practice were attributed to deficiencies in their personal development. In the 'unsupportive' approach, the practice teacher was experienced as cold and aloof. Practice teachers who took a 'constrictive' approach tended to impose their own theoretical viewpoints or even their own ideology on students' work, or provided their own answers, especially at the start, rather than enabling students to discover their own. The fourth 'amorphous' approach was described as lacking in focus and direction, either because ideas were just tossed around without much sense of purpose, or alternatively assignments were gone through mechanically with little exploration. It is disturbing to learn that nearly three-quarters of the students interviewed by Secker towards the end of their third (and final) placement had experienced such unhelpful approaches in one or more of their placements, and almost all of these had not been able to develop the 'fluent practice' described earlier.

This discussion of practice learning in social work education throws up an interesting contrast with its parallel in counselling training, where a greater proportion of the time would probably be spent on one case, and where less attention would be paid to the overall workload, wider issues and accountability to management. Perhaps this is an indication that in both spheres something important is being neglected, and that a better balance might be achieved if each emulated part of the practice of the other.

THEORETICAL LEARNING IN SOCIAL WORK

The debates between different schools of thought – psychodynamic, humanistic, behavioural and so on – so much an issue among those whose primary professional training is in counselling, is not, at least in its finer detail, a major preoccupation for most social workers, whose eclecticism has to be sufficiently broad-ranging to encompass the variety of different roles, tasks and purposes which make up their work. Social workers in training are introduced to a number of different methods and their underpinning theories, and are expected to demonstrate skill in some of them during supervised practice placements. Some of these theories and methods do reflect the schools of thought just mentioned, but at least as much emphasis is likely to be on systems thinking, crisis intervention, task-centred models, radical approaches, empowerment and advocacy, many of which in my experience do not have a high profile in counselling

courses. If we consider the main categories of theory and knowledge used in social work – sociological, psychological, social policy
and organizational – another interesting contrast with counselling
training can be seen in the relative emphasis placed on each source
of understanding. In counselling, a much higher profile tends to be
given to the psychological aspects, those which explain the behaviour of clients and the client–worker interaction, whereas in social
work teaching time is more evenly spread among all the categories.
This reflects social work's greater concern with the social environment of people's lives and the social as well as personal sources of
their problems. Feedback from students on the usefulness of various theoretical areas for their practice, however, gives indications
of more common ground than these contrasts might suggest. Social
work students interviewed by Secker (1993) particularly valued
input on human development, family work, principles of practice
(which offered awareness of values) and interviewing skills. Counselling students, on a course which gave high priority to group
and organizational issues, particularly valued that aspect of their
learning.

In terms of teaching *methods* as opposed to course *content*, both types
of student preferred to experience a range of approaches. Too much
information presented in lecture format was disliked, and there was
resentment if staff did not fully and explicitly acknowledge and
draw on the life experience they brought to the course. Experiential
methods such as role play and simulation exercises were found
helpful because they acted as a bridge between theory and practice
and offered a safe rehearsal ground for skill development. Some
social work courses are now using a thematic approach which
involves students in actively working out what they need to learn
and then exploring a range of resources and sharing their learning
with each other (Burgess and Jackson 1990).

THE COUNSELLING COMPONENT OF SOCIAL WORK
EDUCATION

The main issue for our present purposes is the extent to which
education and training in social work is currently concerned with
inculcating *counselling* skills and understanding. How far does
CCETSW endorse counselling as required learning for competent
social work practice? Do the educational institutions see this as
part of their job? Do the agencies which provide practice teaching
for students offer them an opportunity to develop their skills? Do
newly qualified social work practitioners feel adequately prepared

to undertake counselling where this is required? In theory, the answer to all these questions should be a resounding 'yes!'; the official documents prescribe such aims, and course programmes make strong claims to fulfil these expectations.

The Rules and Requirements for the Diploma in Social Work (CCETSW 1991: 14–19) specifies that qualifying social workers must, among other things, have knowledge and understanding of the:

- aims, methods and theories for practice: counselling, advocacy, negotiation, task-centred work, crisis intervention, family therapy, group living, social education.

Among the interpersonal skills required are the ability to:

- make and sustain working relationships;
- recognize and work with feelings and their impact on themselves and other people;
- recognize and work with aggression, hostility and anger with full consideration of risk to self and others;
- observe, understand and interpret behaviour and attitudes.

This publication also states that qualifying social workers must demonstrate their competence in practice to:

- assess needs, strengths, situations, risks;
- sustain relationships over time with individuals and families and groups;
- help, provide care for, counsel, supervise, protect, individuals and families in difficulties;
- counsel, facilitate, supervise, groups within communities.

These requirements are the ones which have most relevance for the counselling dimension of social work. Yet even this selected group of competencies covers a wider span than is covered in many counselling training courses. Some case illustrations may serve to indicate how necessary it is for those preparing as social workers to learn how to manage the counselling dimension of their role along with a variety of other tasks required by clients, learning which can only be achieved by the broad-ranging and in-depth practice teaching described earlier.

Case illustrations

1. An elderly woman was admitted to a residential home because her daughter, who had been her main carer, was terminally

ill with cancer. A social work student based in the home, who had already got to know her through acting as her key worker, was well-placed to work intensively with her when her daughter died, maintaining a link with relatives, enabling other staff to understand her, offering bereavement counselling, and helping her to consider her future.

2. A young Sikh woman with three very young children was the victim of violent attacks from her husband and as a result her own health was affected and the children seemed to be at risk of both physical and emotional abuse. A social work student, based in the voluntary organization which already knew the family, started by visiting regularly, playing with the children and giving the mother both some respite and a place to air her feelings. Increasing familiarity and trust helped towards a more accurate assessment of the degree of risk involved, and led to the decision to apply for day care for the children. The mother required a great deal of support to negotiate the arrangements with several different professionals, some with racist attitudes, to decide how best to cope with her husband's behaviour, and to elicit whatever support she could from her own community.

These brief examples give an indication of the type of challenge for which social workers are being prepared. It is evident that not only are counselling skills of a high order needed, but also a capacity to integrate these with a range of other types of intervention on the basis of thorough ongoing assessment.

In the light of the powerful directives from CCETSW and the evident client need which these illustrations exemplify, it is salutary to discover that in practice, many newly qualified and even more experienced workers do not feel much confidence in their own counselling skills. Nor do they on the whole experience staff supervision as offering them sufficient chance to build up their competence in this area; on the contrary, it is often done badly or overlooked. Furthermore, many experience their employers as lukewarm in their attitudes to the potential of counselling, to the extent that opportunities are not readily made available to practise in-depth, longer-term work focusing on relationships. There is a danger that these factors taken together can become mutually reinforcing and result in a limited service to those in real need of a counselling approach. On the more positive side, there do exist some encouraging examples of well-supervised creative work, based on good preparation during training, and properly endorsed by the employer.

Illustration: Social work in a hospital burns unit

A social worker meets for the first time the parents of a child just admitted with serious burns. They are in shock, and the implications have not yet sunk in. The nature of help offered at such a time of crisis can make a significant difference in the way the family copes ultimately, so the worker concentrates on establishing a link which will be usable in various ways later. Understanding the medical and nursing care and relating well to these staff members will be vital, as will a grasp of practical ways to support the family, but for the moment building a relationship which they can depend upon is the first priority. The parents are unlikely to have encountered social work before, and are probably unaware of the nature of counselling, so the way the worker gradually conveys the potential of these activities will be important, because it is likely that as treatment progresses, the counselling dimension will become paramount. The worker has to understand the particular environment of the ward and to be aware of the extreme emotional stresses and anxieties such situations evoke in all concerned, staff as well as family. She also needs to have gone some way towards understanding her own reactions to suffering if she is to be of real use to the family. She will need ongoing support from her supervisor, as well as being part of a mutually supportive and cohesive group of staff in the unit, to enable her to stay appropriately involved rather than running away from the pain.

What sort of driving forces and constraints can be identified which might explain some of the difference between flexible, responsive practice like this, and something more superficial and limited? What makes for good practice, and how can the right conditions be fostered? A partial answer to these questions might be gleaned from an examination of the nature of staff supervision in social work.

STAFF SUPERVISION

Practitioners in social work, counselling and psychotherapy all share the conviction that supervision of ongoing work remains crucial long after training is completed. There is, however, much less consensus about what is actually involved in supervision, with a good deal of variation within and between each grouping in terms of definitions, priorities and arrangements.

In social work, 'staff supervision' is the commonly used term, to distinguish it from student supervision or practice teaching.

One predominant theme in the social work literature is the need to ensure that both managerial and professional requirements are met. 'Supervision must have two main purposes; to establish the accountability of the worker to the organisation and to promote the worker's development as a professional person' (DHSS 1978: 200).

The managerial or administrative component is concerned with the implementation of agency policy, the use of resources and standards of work. Supervision in social work is usually the responsibility of the line manager, partly because of the prevailing bureaucratic ethos, and especially because accountability is a key issue. It has to take an overview of the entire workload of the supervisee as well as paying attention to specific pieces of work. It is generally seen as a requirement, and therefore time is allocated for it, although in times of pressure it may well become a casualty, with sessions interrupted or cancelled by crises, despite the fact that it is more than ever needed at such times.

It is arguable that this managerial component has a lower profile in counselling agencies; staff there tend to think single-mindedly of their own clients, and are perhaps not so good at looking at agency policy. As pressures on such agencies grow, it is likely that counsellors will need to give these matters more space in their supervision times.

For professional development the focus is on enabling the worker to cope with the demands of the work, whether by enhancing knowledge and understanding of particular issues in a situation, or by offering support of a more personal nature: '. . . supervision can be a very important part of taking care of oneself, staying open to new learning, and an indispensable part of the helper's ongoing self-development, self-awareness and commitment to learning' (Hawkins and Shohet 1989: 5).

It is probably true to say that counsellors and psychotherapists generally give most emphasis and priority to these educational and supportive components, and in particular to having space to reflect on the content and process of their work and to developing their understanding and skills. Many social workers value these components highly, and seek them out whenever possible. It is likely, however, that a greater proportion of social workers' supervision time will be taken up with boundary issues: Can this family continue to receive a service? Should the responsibility for that case be transferred to another department or agency? Might that individual be eligible for such-and-such a service? Debate about statutory

requirements and interpretation of the law will also have a high
profile in the supervision of social workers, especially those in mental
health, children and family teams and offender work, because of
the degree to which such intervention is underpinned by legislation. Thinking about priorities, resource usage and linkage with
other agencies is likely to take precedence over detailed analysis
of the worker–client relationship, whereas the reverse is true in
agencies dedicated entirely to counselling. It is clear, therefore, that
a major challenge for both types of worker is to achieve a better
balance between these different, often competing but equally vital
components of supervision.

Illustration: Staff supervision in a child abuse case

The inquiry into the death of Kimberley Carlile (Carlile Report
1987) provides a well-publicized example of a breakdown in supervision arrangements which put at risk the protection a child was
entitled to receive. This little girl died of head injuries at the age of
$4^1/2$, having been neglected and physically abused for a very long
period before her death. Her stepfather was convicted of her death
and sentenced to life imprisonment. Both he and her mother were
also convicted of grievous bodily harm. As in all such cases, a highly
complicated sequence of cause-and-effect factors could be teased
out in hindsight. Many individuals and agencies shared responsibility for not averting the tragedy, but the spotlight of blame fell on
the two main fieldworkers – one a social worker, the other a health
visitor – and on their respective line managers for not providing the
active supervision which would have brought to bear an objective
assessment of the case. The social worker in question was a team
leader, new in post, intelligent and conscientious, but overworked
and facing considerable pressures in an under-resourced team. Allocation difficulties had caused him to deal with this case himself.
In these unusual circumstances, arrangements for his own supervision were irregular. His line manager was also under stress, and did
not ensure regular planned times for reporting back on action taken,
reflecting about what was going on, or questioning assessments
made. Because this was seen as such a crucial feature of the mis-
handling of the case, the report discusses at length the nature of
supervision, emphasizing how essential it is, particularly in cases of
child abuse.

Reiterating that the aim of supervision is to help workers gain the
capacity to perform adequately, to enable them to practise to the
best of their ability and to provide as good a service as possible,

the report makes some very convincing remarks about the functions of good supervision:

> Supervision enables practitioners to know themselves . . . The capacity to sit back and have a cool and objective assessment of performance is not a luxury but essential . . . [It] needs to help the social worker recognize the effect achieved by the emotions being beamed out from the family. Many emotions and reactions are contagious . . . While supervision is a skilful and subtle process, supervisors need to be hard-headed and business-like. Effective work . . . requires tangible planning . . . The supervisor also offers evaluation . . . Supervision must be the bedrock which supplies the safeguard that ensures the relevant knowledge is possessed by the practitioner . . . It provides a second opinion.
>
> (Carlile Report 1987: 192–3)

What the report does not cover adequately is the resource implications issue, and in particular the time needed to do the job properly, not only the face-to-face contact, but also the essential reading, reflection and recording. Senior social workers may have oversight of the work of eight or ten staff, and in addition will be covering a range of other management tasks, chairing case conferences, attending policy meetings, contributing to training, liaising with other agencies and scrutinizing new referrals.

Obstacles to good supervision in social work do not derive only from lack of time or from the pressures and crisis-ridden atmosphere described earlier. Part of the problem is that those in line management posts may not have experienced good supervision themselves, and consequently do not feel well-equipped to offer it. Training provision for supervisory roles is patchy, and even where it does exist, it tends to be limited to a couple of days' input with little follow-up. Sad to say, the more senior a person becomes in the hierarchy, the less likely he or she is to encounter good role models in this particular aspect of the work. Without regular experience of the enabling containment offered by high-quality supervision, it is hard to hold onto the motivation and skills required. Gender differences may have an impact on the supervisory process; for example, one research study (Conn 1993) found that female middle managers described their supervisory roles in words like 'supportive', 'advisory', 'empowering', etc., whereas their male counterparts spoke of 'coordinating', 'organizing', 'monitoring'. Another obstacle is the very real difficulty of combining the role of manager with that of supervisor, as explored in the following example.

Illustration: An inter-disciplinary debate about supervision

A group of senior practitioners and first-line managers from social work and nursing backgrounds working mainly in the mental health field were meeting to consider the nature of staff supervision. A fierce debate ensued regarding the appropriateness or otherwise of separating off the functions of managerial accountability from those of professional development, especially in relation to in-depth clinical practice. Some argued that many line managers tended to focus mainly on resource considerations, and that some had little expertise in family dynamics or therapeutic processes. Yet practitioners trying to help extremely damaged and disturbing people require containment for themselves if they are to function effectively; this involves time, attention and a safe place to explore their own feeling responses. Others saw danger in keeping professional and managerial aspects apart from each other. Managers require a familiarity with the workers' competence; they have to monitor the workload, and ensure adequate standards of performance. Workers are supported as much by efficient structures and clear boundaries as by sympathetic listening. As the debate went on, there was a tendency to polarize within the group itself, with some holding on to the more administrative imperatives while others became resistant to these, advocating instead a single-minded concern for developing skills in, and understanding of, the direct encounter with the client. Such 'either/or' reactions indicate that something crucial is at stake, namely the need to reconcile and integrate these apparently conflicting objectives.

At present, attitudes within social work towards supervision tend to be as ambivalent as in this group. The rhetoric about it is positive, but the real support for the thorough provision of a high standard can seem half-hearted. Supervision is likely to be eroded as pressure to cut costs grows in tandem with increasing demands on the limited staff resources available. However, as Dearnley (1985: 55) points out:

> . . . agencies concerned with public safety and accountability, such as Social Services Departments, let supervision go at their peril . . . focussed, detailed supervision is what sustains, contains and enables learning and ensures the agency's safety by developing good practice . . . if supervision only deals with crises and management issues, the worker is likely so to deal with clients, and the clients in their turn come to expect only

a first-aid service . . . the agency becomes labelled as a casualty service staffed by casualty workers, and can never deal with underlying problems.

Despite all these dilemmas and the undoubted inadequacies in much current practice, there do exist some profound insights from the practice and writing of social workers who use a psychodynamic frame of reference; ideas which, if they were more widely disseminated and utilized, could make a real contribution towards improving standards of supervision not only in social work but also wherever counselling is practised. The following statement serves well as an introduction to such ideas:

Supervision is a safe place where the worker together with his supervisor examines the dynamics of the family and its relationship with and within the community; he can examine his own relationship with and feelings about the family and can use this information to determine the nature of presenting problems, areas of work and methods of work and future goals for that family. The interactive process between the supervisor and worker can often be a useful tool in this task.

(Blech 1981: 7)

A valuable concept, 'the reflection process', is being referred to here, the notion that 'the processes at work currently in the *relationship between* client and worker are often reflected in the *relationship between* worker and supervisor' (Mattinson 1975: 11). At the Institute of Marital Studies at the Tavistock Clinic, Mattinson and her colleagues had gradually learned about the potential value of picking up and using this reflection or 'mirroring' in supervision. The process usually manifests itself not in a logical verbal way, but in uncharacteristic behaviour or attitudes of the worker in the supervision session. These could easily be misconstrued by the supervisor as unhelpful, stupid or defiant, for example, until on further examination it is discovered that they actually convey very vividly some aspect of the client's functioning which has been too disturbing or too mystifying to communicate directly. Unravelling the process in supervision can then offer a useful insight into what is going on between worker and client, an insight which might otherwise have remained inaccessible.

Supervision is not only concerned with direct one-to-one client–worker transactions, but equally with relationships between workers of different professional backgrounds and those at different levels in the hierarchy, and not least with attitudes and communication among different agencies and organizations. Again, psychodynamic thinking can help us to understand and work better with some of the complicated issues which arise whenever people attempt to work collaboratively across boundaries. This is the subject of the next chapter.

FIVE

Professional relationships in counselling in social work

A crucial aspect of social work practice is the nature and extent of the communication, linkages, negotiations and shared work with those in other disciplines and departments. These interfaces have at least as much impact on the counselling dimension of the work as does any other single factor. There has never been greater need for flexible and effective cooperation across the boundaries of profession and agency. This is partly due to heightened stress in the community, causing families to experience a multiplicity of needs which can only be met by a range of services acting in conjunction. Agencies themselves change their focus and methods of work, developing fresh specialisms or reaching out to different users. Wider social change is reflected in new legislation and social policy, altered expectations of help, and shifts in the relative position of the state, private and voluntary sectors of care. Furthermore, one of the main grounds for criticism of social work has been its failure to develop skills in working with other disciplines and professions.

I will give some examples first of the quantity and range of social workers' connectedness with others. With which other professionals and agencies do social workers most frequently work? What sorts of shared tasks do they undertake? How are these carried out, and with what aims? The complex multifaceted nature of the resulting working relationships are then explored. What obstacles are encountered? Why should such sharing often give rise to an extreme degree of difficulty, conflict and stress? What concepts might help towards a better understanding of the very serious state of affairs which pertains in much collaborative work in the helping professions? In particular, what impact does this have on the counselling dimension of social work, and how might insights from counselling contribute towards the resolution of problems of collaboration? Also, I ask whether social workers' experiences of working across boundaries offer any help to counsellors in other settings.

A recent study of working relationships across professions and agencies as well as at an interpersonal level provides a useful conceptual framework for examining collaboration among the vast number of those in the helping services who need to coordinate their provision. Apart from *primary collaboration*, which is about the relationships between and shared responsibilities of worker and client, two other types of shared work are identified which specifically concern us here:

> *Secondary collaboration* describes the relationships of several helpers working together for the benefit of a user, without the latter present. *Participatory collaboration* describes the complexity of individual and group relationships that occur when the user is present and taking part, however minimally.
>
> (Hornby 1993: 42)

The purpose of this shared work is to provide optimum help, by integrating methods and coordinating services to meet particular needs. Hornby also draws attention to a problem fundamental to all communication, that of terminology. The fact that each profession necessarily uses language in its own particular way, without recognizing the different meanings and nuances given by others to the same words, means that misunderstandings are unwittingly built into an interdisciplinary encounter from the start. Hornby attempts to establish common ground by introducing a new basic collaborative vocabulary, for example by using the term 'faceworker' for helpers at ground level, 'care-compact' for methods of care integrated to meet the needs of a particular user, and 'trouble' for whatever brings a user to seek help. However, this perhaps poses the same difficulties as Esperanto did to world languages – how many people will learn the new vocabulary? – otherwise it becomes yet another tongue to add to the tower of Babel.

INTERFACES IN SOCIAL WORK

Referral and intake

Requests for social work help may come directly from the public. They also come from the whole spectrum of health, educational and judicial services, together with those statutory departments and voluntary agencies concerned with issues relating to housing, welfare rights, marital problems and all sorts of personal and family malaise. Both counsellors and workers with a counselling dimension in their role are therefore likely to form a significant proportion of those making referrals to social workers.

As discussed in Chapter Two, the fact that these demands for intervention far exceed the supply of resources forces social workers into rationing and gate-keeping roles. Such pressure is partly due to the progressive heightening of expectations resulting from successive pieces of legislation and expansion of services over the last twenty-five years, and much in evidence today in relation to care in the community. The notion that provision should be universally available to meet all sorts of social needs is now seen to be over-ambitious and unrealistic, but it is an assumption which tends to persist; and especially in the face of contraction of provision, it is social workers who tend to be blamed and scapegoated when they cannot produce the goods.

The intake boundary which social workers have to manage is extremely wide and exposed. Woodhouse and Pengelly (1991) point out that it is therefore no wonder that they speak of the 'bombardment rate' of referrals, and see themselves as being the 'dustbin' for everyone else's problems. They regard their department as a 'citadel under siege whose occupants kept an ever watchful eye on the portal' (p. 231). This 'embattled stance' can be described as one in which practitioners and managers try to ensure that others do not pass the buck. This can result not infrequently in some dishonesty in referrals made for social work services, for example a less than full picture of all the dimensions of a situation, or exaggeration of its urgency. The anxiety endemic in this scenario, the defences it gives rise to, and the consequences for professional relationships will be discussed in more detail later.

Information sharing

Unlike those working in counselling agencies, social workers spend a great deal of time eliciting information and responding to requests from others for information about their clients. This is largely because of the major statutory component in the social work role, and the consequent large number of reports which have to be produced. Checking whether other agencies are involved in a particular situation, clarifying the respective roles of different workers, gauging the degree of concern felt about a problem, finding out

about availability of resources, attempting to gain further understanding of the background, and planning the next stage of intervention are all examples of normal practice in social work. Child
protection work provides the ultimate illustration of the need for
such sharing:

> It is vital, if full collaborative effort is to be maintained in child
> protection, that the main agencies fully exchange all the rel-
> evant knowledge they have. To maintain bits of information in
> disparate documentary sources that are not collated is to handi-
> cap those who need to rely on optimum information.
>
> (Carlile Report 1987: 89)

Along with reports, written records provide a particular illustration of information sharing dilemmas in social work. Records are
kept for a variety of purposes – legal, managerial and professional
– and in the fulfilment of these some incompatibility is often
experienced, both between agency requirements and those of
the worker, and in the amount of detail, balance of fact, opinion
and hypothesis included. It is often essential, for example in child
protection work, to record exactly when visits were made, what
precisely was observed and what action taken. For the worker's
own thinking and for the professional development component
of staff supervision, it is helpful to have the freedom to be more
impressionistic, to speculate about cause-and-effect links, and to
comment on what might have been done differently. For effective
monitoring of resource provision, the extent of *unmet* need should
in theory be recorded in a form susceptible to statistical analysis.

The Data Protection Act 1984 and the Access to Personal Files Act
1987 gave clients the right of access to their records. It is necessary,
although not always easy, to judge when limited access is required,
for example when accumulating information in order to make a
case for legal action, or when confidentiality between different family members is needed. There are indications that open access has
the potential to bring real benefits – a more open approach, better
sharing of assessments, plans and decisions, greater empowerment
of clients and safeguarding of their rights, and clearer, better-
evidenced, more focused records (Doel and Lawson 1986).

Verbal information-sharing can be a minefield of problems, and
to some extent seems to run counter to fundamental principles in
counselling, in particular the maintenance of confidentiality and
full client consent to any communication about their situation with
a third party. Social workers struggle to balance their responsibilities to clients and to others involved in the situation, trying

to identify the right principles to inform their day-to-day decisions about what to communicate and what to withhold. A great deal is at stake; if this fine balance is not judged accurately, the price to be paid may be a client's sense of betrayal, or a wrong decision based on partial knowledge, or a poor relationship with a resource-provider, or the risk of being judged culpable in a potentially life-threatening situation.

Biestek (1961) explains how very complex this principle of confidentiality is and how difficult it is to apply to concrete situations. In both social work and the medical professions, the client's secret information is being communicated not only to the worker but also to the agency, in effect making it a group secret: 'the biggest difficulty concerning the ethical use of the group secret is the establishment of a policy concerning intra-agency and extra-agency divulgence of secret information' (Biestek 1961: 126). Necessary for this is the weighing of conflicting rights against an awareness of the overriding common good.

Illustration: A mental health tragedy

In early 1994, a young mother, Sharon Dalson, was found guilty of killing her two young children nearly two years previously, and was confined indefinitely in a high-security hospital. The family had been known to both the police and social services in Haringey since 1988, when the children, then babies, had occasionally been left alone. After a period of apparent calm, neighbours expressed concern about the children, police investigated, the mother was charged with assault on her son, the children's names were placed once again on the 'at risk' register, and they were put in the care of the maternal grandmother. After another interlude, not long before the children died, their mother was seen by psychiatrists and compulsorily detained in hospital under the Mental Health Act because of her psychotic behaviour. It was during a further episode of her psychosis that she killed the children. In the aftermath of investigation, publicity and recrimination, it emerged that social workers 'never saw' police statements about the mother's earlier violence, and likewise, police called to the house to investigate were unaware that the children were on the register. The precise reasons for this were unclear, but fear of infringing parents' civil liberties and breakdown of cooperation between council and police at the time were suggested as possible explanations. This case certainly highlights how crucial is good communication between all involved; neighbours and psychiatric services as well as police and social workers all possessed vital pieces of information, which, if shared and put together, could possibly have averted the tragedy. Otherwise, the right preventive and therapeutic measures could not even be initiated, far less properly carried out.

Participation in case conferences

Precisely to address the type of situation just outlined, and especially, though not exclusively, where there is a serious concern about child protection, a case conference may be called.

> The primary purpose of case conferences is to act as a vehicle for inter-agency work. The case conference members attempt to ensure that all the relevant information is pooled, and that the case will be handled on a multi-agency, multidisciplinary basis. Professional perspectives will be shared, with a view to protecting the child, assessing the situation and planning future work.
>
> (Stainton Rogers *et al.* 1989: 190)

Attempts to work simultaneously across the boundaries both of agencies and of professions mean that problems of difference, whether of basic training, frame of reference, language, central focus of work, priorities, values or resources, are likely to be amplified. Since the issue is almost always a distressing one with a large element of risk, the ordinary challenges of stating one's own thoughts coherently, of relating to others who may well have different priorities and opposite points of view, and of finding a mutually agreed way forward, all have to be carried out in an atmosphere fraught with tension, a sense of crisis or emergency, and very powerful emotions. Developed skills in convening and chairing meetings are essential for such complex collaborative work – resolving questions of format and representation, enabling all present to share their thoughts and feelings, coping with misunderstanding and conflict, and steering the group towards good decisions. The management of complex group dynamics is a skill which is not necessarily gained in the basic training of social workers – or indeed of most other professional groups – but nowhere is the need for it more in evidence than in the anxiety-ridden climate of a case conference. Commenting on the difficult task facing case conferences of assessing the degree of risk in the lives of abused children, the Report of the Jasmine Beckford Inquiry states:

> The overriding consideration of case conferences is that they should inject into the process of decision-making an objectivity

that cannot be obtained by those directly involved in the management of a child abuse case . . . Bringing together a mixture of professional disciplines may not achieve the desired objectivity; indeed the larger the spread of disciplines the more unwieldy . . . and the more muffled will be the message.

(Beckford Report 1985: 250–51)

We now have some well-documented instances in which the case conference actually added to the abuse of the child and the distress of the family instead of achieving anything positive.

Illustration: A problematic case conference

Bacon (1988) describes in detail the ways in which a particular case conference, and the individual professionals in it, got into a mess with a family. The problem was that a five-year-old boy, one of three children in a very disturbed family, was being seriously emotionally abused. The childminder, general practitioner (GP) and headmistress all offered information about a very sad, rejected, deteriorating child. Those in social services agreed entirely with the facts as presented, and the social worker became key-worker by mutual agreement, but problems arose when the whole group tried to decide what precise action was required. They struggled with issues like how honest to be with the parents, and whether direct work should be done with the boy, and did not achieve any clear answers. It seemed that each professional felt the knowledge they possessed to be explosive, dangerous and liable to cause the family's relationship with potential helpers to break down, or alternatively to bring about more violence and damage within the family. They also feared that they would become fragmented from each other, a fear that was actually realized when they could not agree about the need for the family to be placed on the child abuse register. Ideally, the conference should have offered a clear sense of direction and enabled those workers who had to take difficult steps to feel authorized by their colleagues to act. Instead, there was confusion, resentment towards those with different points of view, and some fudged decisions. In the end, it was the child who suffered even more, as his needs for someone to get close to him and to pay serious attention to his predicament got overlaid by the way the professionals took flight from the primitive anxieties raised by the case, and collectively colluded in keeping their distance.

As Archer and Whitaker (1992: 68) point out: 'Conferences meant to focus on child or family contain covertly expressed attempts to deal with the anxieties and concerns of the participants.' In Cleveland, 'processes and procedures intended to protect children and promote their welfare degenerated into instruments of depersonalisation, and . . . practitioners distanced themselves from the relevant adults' (Woodhouse and Pengelly 1991: 245).

Other inter-agency work

Case conferences are just one facet of a much larger arena of work across agency boundaries, and the Cleveland Inquiry provides further insight into the problems faced. The inquiry was the first to look at how all the agencies in a given locality worked together in a range of sexual abuse cases, not just a single tragedy. The main professional groupings involved were paediatricians, social workers and police, each with their own distinctive concerns, methods of working and organizational pressures. For example, the methods of working and need for sound evidence required by the police in order to investigate crime and bring prosecutions were not held in mind by paediatricians preoccupied with diagnosis, or by social workers trying to assess the safety of children. It is evident that all these are complementary tasks with the potential to be of mutual benefit, but in the extreme pressure of the crisis it was the divergence of priorities which was paramount, to the great detriment of working relationships and appropriate action. Subjective feelings about each others' roles also played a part; for example, the director of social work and the child abuse consultant felt unable to challenge the validity of the diagnostic findings of the paediatricians, even in terms of their implications for child-care decision-making. In trying to pinpoint the complex reasons for the crisis, the inquiry's conclusions particularly mentioned the following:

- lack of a proper understanding by the main agencies of each others' functions;
- a lack of communication between the agencies;
- differences of views at middle management level.

(Butler-Sloss 1988: 243)

The social workers in Cleveland were undoubtedly affected by previous child abuse inquiries which had castigated social workers for failing to take sufficiently prompt and decisive action on the basis of the findings of others. But now the pendulum had swung too far the other way, resulting in hasty and ill-considered action.

A lesson to be learned from the 1980s is that inter-agency working is not easy, and not self evidently useful. That is not to say that an agency can go it alone, but separate viewpoints and confusion of roles, as well as the availability of multiple pathways for communication, are a recipe for muddle.

(Department of Health 1991: 41)

Fortunately, there do exist examples of more positive practice. These include some creative shared work in community mental health teams and community mental handicap teams. Child protection teams are beginning to involve new levels of cooperation between police and social workers, especially in sensitive joint interviewing of children making disclosures about abuse, aimed at preventing them from having to repeat the description of painful experiences to various people in succession.

Teams and multidisciplinary teamwork

Øvretveit (1993: 55, 9) defines a *team* as 'a small group of people who relate to each other to contribute to a common goal', and a *multidisciplinary team* as 'a group of practitioners with different professional training . . . who meet regularly to coordinate their work providing services to one or more clients in a defined area'. Sporting analogies are often used to highlight differences between teams of different types. In athletics or tennis, there is more emphasis on individual excellence contributing in its own right to the final outcome; the work of most counsellors, and that of social workers dealing with some of their own allocated cases, is of this type. By contrast, in hockey or football, each team member's skills have to be fully integrated with those of all others for the common good. This is the case with social workers functioning together in a duty system, receiving new work and responding to emergencies, passing on information and initial assessments to colleagues for further action, or sharing the tasks in a crisis situation (Hillman and Mackenzie 1993). Teams comprising different disciplines bear even greater resemblance to this more integrated type, because of the variety of specialist skills and positions involved, and the need to develop shared strategies of approach to particular situations.

Practically all social workers are located in teams within their own profession and agency, and a significant proportion of them also function at least part of the time as a member of a multidisciplinary team, both within and beyond their own agency boundaries. For example, a large psychiatric hospital may have deployed within

it a sizeable group of social workers, employed by the local authority to carry out statutory mental health duties and a range of other
functions. Each worker is likely to have specific responsibilities in
a particular department of the hospital and to function as an integral
part of that health care team along with doctors, nurses, psychologists
and others. This dual membership sometimes brings about a sense
of divided loyalties, especially where priorities are at variance. A
powerful contributor to professional self-esteem and role identity is
the feeling of belonging to a cohesive group of people who share
day-to-day work, and when this group comprises members of the
various disciplines in a ward or department rather than other social
work colleagues, then formal social work team meetings may seem
irrelevant to the task.

As far as the counselling dimension of multidisciplinary work is
concerned, great sensitivity is required to establish quickly a relationship of trust not only between the client and the individual
worker, but also between the client and the team. This involves the
worker acting not simply as an autonomous counselling practitioner
but also as a representative of the team or agency and a mediator
of its services. The challenge of such roles is to convey to the client
a clear sense of what others may be able to offer with reasons for
their possible involvement, and at the same time to avoid giving a
message of rejection or confusion.

Trans-disciplinary work – family therapy

Social workers based in multidisciplinary teams, especially (but by
no means exclusively) those in child, adolescent and family psychiatry, are very likely to engage in 'family therapy'. From a counselling perspective this could be regarded as part of the wider sphere
of 'family counselling', and from a social work vantage point it is
one segment of the large component of the job labelled 'social work
with families'. Family therapy is a specialist area of work with its
own principles, methodology and literature, which over the last
twenty years or so have been built up jointly by a range of disciplines including psychiatry, psychology, nursing and occupational
therapy as well as social work. As such, it provides a particularly
interesting example of *trans*-disciplinary work (Burnham 1986).
Many of those practising family therapy use systems thinking, which
was discussed at the beginning of Chapter Two (Skynner 1976,
Walrond-Skinner 1981, Preston-Shoot and Agass 1990). A number
of key principles, shared by all the professionals involved, form the
basis for work done with the family. For example, cause-and-effect

links in the problem are not seen as linear (A causes B to behave in a particular way), but rather as circular (B influences and is influenced by A and others in ways only understood in the whole context of their interaction). Problems are not seen as residing in a given individual but instead as the product of relationships in the whole system. As far as possible, therefore, the whole family is seen together from the start. In addition, several members of the team may cooperate in work with that family, for example by observing the session through a one-way screen and engaging in 'live' consultancy or supervision as it proceeds. Because both the understanding of the problem and also the means of addressing it are to a large extent held in common by all team members, their roles tend to be interchangeable rather than clearly demarcated along traditional lines of hierarchy or professional discipline. What is found to be vital for the success of this way of working is to give ample time and careful attention to the relationships of the workers as well as to family dynamics and interview processes (Treacher and Carpenter 1984).

Relationships with those in management and policy-making roles

Referring to the turmoil produced by cutbacks, uncertain futures and heavy demands, Coulshed (1990: 1) says:

> As a result of these pressures occasionally it has seemed that our large systems have acted as if people do not matter. More and more I meet social workers, particularly in the statutory sector, who feel powerless at work; they cynically scoff at the notion that part of their role is to question procedures, shape policy or improve services. A number of staff appear alienated, especially from senior managers who seem to place increasing emphasis on management technologies.

This statement highlights a destructive tendency for those at different levels in the hierarchy to grow apart and to feel split off from each others' central concerns. As we saw previously in the debate about inter-agency work, these concerns are opposite sides of the same coin, each essential and complementary to the other, however incompatible they may feel. Managers and policy makers need to be in touch with the needs of service users, and to monitor the effectiveness or otherwise of their decisions; grassroots workers are the ones who possess this knowledge. Likewise, the workers most in contact with users need to understand, and if possible to share in, the thinking behind decisions about resources, deployment of staff, procedural guidelines and other management issues. Mutual respect and a range of effective means of communication between the two groups are therefore vital. Why should these so often be lacking? An example from a very small new agency exemplifies some of the divisive processes in operation.

Illustration: Staff–management conflict in a new project

A service came into being to meet some of the mental health needs in a community. A management committee with good representation from the locality was set up, funding obtained and premises found. Staff with social work and community education backgrounds were appointed. Their responsibility was to develop outreach work, to link with other services and to offer counselling and groupwork. Trouble started after the first few weeks of work, when staff asked how precisely they should convey their experiences to management – whether by attendance at management committee meetings, by writing reports or through the project leader. This seemingly innocuous and appropriate request provoked a very strong hostile reaction in the committee and especially in its chairman. He experienced staff as threatening his decision-making power and usurping his role. Other committee members, especially those new to the group, felt uncertain and confused, as they had not yet got to know each other and the way the project worked. Bad feeling (and bad behaviour) escalated quickly, leaving everyone angry and hurt and the service at risk of total breakdown. What seemed to have happened was that the wish to share findings had been misconstrued as a takeover bid, and weaknesses in the system such as personality clashes and power struggles arising from differences of gender, experience and role became, against everyone's better judgement, more dominant than the central aims of the work.

REASONS FOR DIFFICULTY IN COLLABORATIVE WORK AND CONCEPTS TO HELP UNDERSTANDING

It would be a relatively simple matter to list the many obstacles to effective work across agency and professional boundaries, but such a list would do little justice to the complexity of the real world, where each of the difficulties affects and is affected by a range of others to form intricate or cause-and-effect linkages and chains of reaction. An attempt will be made to demonstrate this dynamic interaction in the discussion which follows. A further important consideration is that this is an area where logical and rational factors may well have less impact than unconscious forces – hidden agendas, primitive processes and the like. As Morgan (1986: 199) puts it in his exploration of the notion of organizations as psychic prisons:

> This metaphor joins the idea that organizations are psychic phenomena, in the sense that they are ultimately created and sustained by conscious and unconscious processes, with the notion that people can actually become imprisoned or confined by the images, ideas, thoughts, and actions to which these processes give rise.

The role of anxiety

Counsellors are extremely familiar with the destructive impact that anxiety, particularly in its most primitive unconscious forms, has on the behaviour and relationships of individuals. What is now being increasingly recognized is that those self-same sorts of anxiety can have equally damaging effects upon groups and organizations; these effects can be seen particularly clearly in troubled interactions within and between professions and agencies (Menzies-Lyth 1988, 1989; Brearley 1989; Woodhouse and Pengelly 1991; Hornby 1993). When levels of anxiety become intolerably painful, normal functioning is seriouly affected, and there arises a pressing need to construct defences or protective mechanisms in order to survive and cope. *Denial* is one of the most familiar defences, a common device to keep unpleasant reality at bay. *Splitting*, the extreme polarization of experiences into good and bad, idealized and hated, is a defence used to manage the anxiety related to the seeming impossibility of dealing simultaneously with utterly contradictory feelings. It is very often encountered in inter-agency and inter-professional work when, for example, a client seems to be driving a wedge between various workers by disparaging one and confiding secrets in another; processes described in graphic detail by Mattinson and Sinclair (1979). Another defence frequently in operation in organizational life is *projection*, ascribing some of one's own unwanted characteristics to others – 'the pot calling the kettle black'. Calling this the *downing defence*, Hornby (1993: 123) says:

> In this process the unacceptable attribute is projected on to another worker or agency which is 'downed' so that another worker or agency may be correspondingly 'upped'. This defence protects against role insecurity when the worker's self-image as a competent practitioner is under threat.

Why should such a powerful role be played by anxiety and its associated defences in working partnerships across agency and professional boundaries? A major reason, according to Menzies-Lyth (1988, 1989), is that these mechanisms can permeate whole institutional structures, cultures and ways of working, to an extent that successive staff members experience them as 'givens' in the system and feel powerless to change them; indeed, they may be hardly aware of them in any explicit way. Basing her thinking on extensive action research in hospitals, she shows how the deep anxieties confronted, for example, by nurses in their work – fears of dependency, mutilation, death – can find expression in habitual modes of relationship between senior and junior nurses, in depersonalizing ways of referring to patients, such as 'the pneumonia in bed 15', in ritual task-performance, and in many other behaviours. One serious problem about institutionalized defences is that, although they come into being as a necessary means of coping, they then tend to become problems in their own right, causing long-term disturbance in functioning and relationships.

Further insights into processes of this sort are provided by Woodhouse and Pengelly (1991) in a book entitled *Anxiety and the Dynamics of Collaboration*. Practitioners of different sorts – GPs, health visitors, marriage counsellors, social workers and probation officers – met in special workshops over a three-year period. Members regularly presented work with their current cases, and part of the task was to examine ways of improving working relationships across disciplines and agencies. What emerged very clearly was that in addition to all the expected anxieties and defences generated by the predicaments of their patients and clients, the practitioners are also very much subject to task-related anxieties specific to their own particular agency and profession. The resulting unconscious defences become a major factor in preventing effective collaboration. The study identifies the key anxiety-provoking issues for each profession which lead to characteristic defensive ways of functioning, and demonstrates how these give rise to particular sorts of problematic interaction.

It is likely that these complex processes constitute a significant factor in the various sorts of collaborative difficulty that I now describe.

Inter-agency myths, stereotyping and rivalry

Because of the increasingly complex nature of the network of helping agencies, it is inevitable that there is a great deal of ignorance about the exact function of each one. Not all agencies have a clear, readily communicable identity which enables others to use them most appropriately. Even when basic facts, such as aims, client group served, main resources and types of approach are known, many other less tangible bits of information, such as the particular style of work and the precise sort of problem most effectively dealt with, is harder to come by. When lack of knowledge of this sort is compounded by lack of understanding of the roles of the various professions who comprise the staff of an agency, the stage is set for some primitive reactions towards each other's work. Myths and fantasies flourish in a climate of ignorance. Stereotypes held about a particular agency or discipline tend to become more limited, inaccurate and pejorative in the absence of opportunities to correct and update them. In turn, the interactions based on these misperceptions are liable to become conflictual rather than cooperative, with the risk of a vicious spiral of distancing, mistrust and disparagement coming into operation. When the players in this drama are themselves under pressure, lacking in confidence, threatened by possible invidious comparisons and criticisms, and unsupported, then rivalry, envy and breakdown in relationships may result.

Illustration

A very small primary school with residential facilities is run by a voluntary organization to cater for children who cannot cope in the ordinary school system. Because these children are among the most damaged and disturbed of their age group, and because work is also done with their families, the school has a high staffing ratio and is relatively generously resourced in other ways. The staff (teachers and social workers) try to work closely with educational psychologists, local authority social workers and teachers in the mainstream schools to ensure that children's needs are fully understood and that agreements are reached about the most appropriate plans for them. One of the main obstacles to effective cooperation seems to be considerable envy of the school's apparently luxurious provision on the part of the outside professionals. This is frequently getting in the way of creative collaboration in helping a child with special needs. 'It's all very well for you, but I have thirty other children to attend to, and I can't afford to spend all this time and effort on just one of them!' says one teacher due to take over a child ready to move from the special school. Likewise, some of the community-based social workers are reluctant to engage in joint family work or to incorporate the insights of school staff into their plans, apparently because it might highlight the limitations of what they were able to offer – certainly their own resources and support systems leave a lot to be desired. Review meetings (attended by parents) sometimes unfortunately become a forum for the subtle expression of distrust between school staff and educational psychologist. The result is that workers in different locations and disciplines drift apart from each other, with a sense of mutual resentment replacing the complementarity and mutual dependence which the situation requires. As one of the school social workers remarks, 'It is the children and parents who are the main losers – together we could offer them so much more – it's really sad!'

As new needs in the community are identified, and a variety of services comes into being in response, there is a risk that ignorance, suspicion and uncertainty about the value of one's own as yet not firmly established role will combine to cause a particularly unfortunate sort of territorial rivalry among both agencies and individual staff working in that particular area of work. This process can sometimes be discerned for example in the wake of a major disaster, where counselling on a large scale may be needed, and various professional groupings, such as social workers, clergy, GPs, psychologists, psychiatrists and counsellors in voluntary organizations are all wishing to offer their services. It is ironic that there is more than enough work for everyone, but the crisis atmosphere and absence of tried and tested coordinating mechanisms can make it seem as if each group has to fight for its place. Often a climate of mutual criticism comes into being, instead of the desired support and complementarity. A similar problem is experienced in the HIV and AIDS field, where the need for agencies to compete for funding complicates the difficulty still further. It is significant that in both these instances the nature of the work itself is exceptionally anxiety-provoking, and it is therefore not surprising that agencies and professional groupings as well as individuals respond in defensive ways.

The 'collusion of anonymity'

A valuable insight into one aspect of cooperation and shared responsibility is offered by Balint (1964). His concern is with the professional relationships of GPs, but his ideas are equally applicable to any group in the helping professions which refers its clients to others while continuing the relationship and maintaining some responsibility for the overall situation. The process is as follows. The original worker asks a colleague in another agency or discipline for specialist help. This colleague perceives a further way of tackling part of the problem, and in turn refers on to someone else, and so on. If this sequence is repeated without adequate feedback and follow-up, 'Vital decisions are taken without anybody feeling fully responsible for them' (Balint 1964: 76) The central person – the patient or client – is more than likely to be confused by the various suggestions or offers, and even worse, may feel some loss of identity as each successive helper focuses on one part of the situation without giving due weight to the whole picture. A GP usually receives reports enabling him or her to keep some track of the process, and has the chance to see the patient on return visits. This is less likely to be the case in other professions. There may have been an agreement about a particular person acting as key worker, but without good communication and efficient procedures for review, such agreements become out-of-date, not subscribed to by all concerned, or else subject to inaccurate assumptions and sheer ignorance.

WAYS OF ENHANCING COLLABORATIVE WORK

How can the skills, understanding and preparedness to work co-operatively be given adequate attention in the professional development of all those who require such competence? A number of strategies are identified, with examples and discussion of each.

Basic training

There is some evidence that this area is given relatively low priority in qualifying training for social work. Even CCETSW, whose requirements are generally presented in detail, gives little explicit emphasis to collaboration. For example, out of well over a hundred core areas of knowledge, skill and competence required by qualifying social workers, only five specifically deal with professional relationships:

- understand the structures of central and local government, the criminal justice system, and other relevant statutory, voluntary and private bodies, and their inter-relationships;
- be able to negotiate, network, work in partnership;
- be able to make decisions where collaboration with other agencies and professionals is necessary;
- be able to contribute to the formulation of programmes of care in collaboration with users, carers and other professions;

- understand and where necessary take part in procedures for inter-professional collaboration:

(CCETSW 1991: 17–19)

Certainly such skills are needed, but the problem with this short catalogue is that it simply does not go far enough. In particular, it does not take into account the need for mutuality and for an in-depth grasp of the emotional complexity of working across boundaries with the anxiety-provoking material which is the stuff of helping work.

Periods of assessed practice, complemented by experiential teaching methods like role-play, are likely to be the chief means through which social work students at the qualifying stage build up their experience and develop their confidence in working with others. The fact that a placement in the final stage of training must comprise at least eighty days over a period of six months or more, means that there is a good opportunity to develop ongoing contacts. If practice teachers can enable students to reflect on the nuances of their various encounters and support them in critically evaluating their own part in the transactions experienced, then an openness and sensitivity to the perspectives of others gradually becomes part of their professional repertoire.

Because there is a good deal of common ground among all the helping professions, especially about the need for a basic understanding of human growth and behaviour, the acquisition of core skills in making enabling relationships, and exploration of the value base of the work, it would make a lot of sense if these areas could be studied in an interdisciplinary context from an early stage in professional training. It is sad, therefore, that perennial attempts to achieve this have tended to founder on grounds of allegedly incompatible timetables and academic requirements. However, a survey by Storrie (1992) indicated that degree courses focusing on inter-professional understanding are at last beginning to be established in significant numbers.

What is the equivalent position in counselling training? Because a much smaller component of the work is concerned with collaboration, it is likely that this area receives even less attention. The danger then is that even experienced counsellors may feel some uncertainty in both initiating and responding to contact from other disciplines about their clients. The Cleveland Inquiry's statement that there is a need for inter-agency training and recognition of the role of other disciplines is certainly applicable to counselling. The inclusion of input from social workers, psychiatrists and GPs in the training of marriage counsellors is an example of positive practice, one which has the added benefit of familiarizing members of those professions with the potential of such counselling. Counselling courses that are attended by experienced workers from the whole spectrum of helping professions have a tailor-made opportunity to foster better understanding, which could probably be exploited more explicitly by the incorporation of inter-agency collaboration into the syllabus.

Post-qualifying training and shared courses and workshops

Opportunities for full-scale post-qualifying training are relatively scarce, and it is not always easy to find adequate funding. However, in 1992 there were forty-seven CCETSW-approved post-qualifying study programmes involving 355 social workers, together with a significant number of people from other professions on some of the courses. These programmes offer a chance for experienced workers to acquire new knowledge and skills, to reflect on their practice and in some instances to undertake small research projects. These can provide good opportunities for intensive learning about collaborative work, because both the course membership and the content of learning may have multidisciplinary aspects. For example, one post-qualifying social work student had several months' well-supervised practice in bereavement counselling in a health centre. This involved her in working out her specific contribution in relation to all the various disciplines represented in the centre and in undertaking some conjoint work. It would be most helpful if a proportion of social workers could have opportunities like this relatively early in their career, before constricted patterns of shared work have a chance to become too firmly established, and before they move away from direct practice into management or training roles.

There exists a plethora of short courses and in-service training opportunities in social work and related fields. If these can be offered on an inter-disciplinary and inter-agency basis, there is tremendous potential for building mutual understanding and trust, and dispelling the myths which various professional groups have about each other.

Illustration

In an area of multiple deprivation, a small voluntary organization acted as the catalyst to set up some introductory courses on child

abuse, using Open University materials. It was attended by representatives of many of the different professions working in the area.
The participants undertook to do their own substantial private study,
and came together as a group at weekly intervals for three months,
for discussion of theoretical material, skill development using video
triggers and experiential exercises, clarification of roles, and mutual
support for the emotional demands of the work. Those taking part
included nursery nurses, school nurses and health visitors, nursery,
primary and secondary school teachers, social workers from field
and residential settings, staff from voluntary organizations and
police. Each group offered feedback at the end of their course and,
without exception, the greatest benefit they experienced was the
cross-fertilization and understanding of each other's roles, ways of
working, attitudes and dilemmas. All this had an immediate effect
on their working practices. There was then a strong impetus to use
a similar format for in-service training on communication with
children.

Consultancy

When working relationships are strained, it is often helpful to look
at what is going wrong with the help of an objective outsider.
Process consultancy is the involvement of someone with no vested
interests, a skilled listener with understanding of group and organizational dynamics, who can comment on underlying cause-and-
effect factors in the problem, and support the group members in
arriving at more constructive perceptions and behaviour.

Illustrations

1. A multidisciplinary team in adolescent psychiatry made use
of external consultancy on a monthly basis over a long period. A
recurrent theme was the tension in working relations brought about
by power imbalances, as between, for example, doctors and nurses,
men and women, or long-standing and newer members of staff.
The greater value given to the views of, say, psychologists over
teachers or occupational therapists was another issue, as was the
different priority given to certain aspects of the work by social
workers compared with other staff. Because there was a regular
opportunity to reflect on and understand the conflictual feelings
and behaviour engendered by these differences, there was less risk
of such rivalries becoming a permanent and destructive feature of
the functioning of the whole team. They were thus more able to

think creatively about the therapeutic needs of patients and families, and to act as more effective co-workers in groups. They were also able to withstand the debilitating effect of chronic uncertainty about the future of the whole unit when they could face it together rather than in factions.

2. A large voluntary social work organization regularly makes provision for all the staff in a given project to spend a day together periodically, away from their usual work base, and often facilitated by an external consultant. They are thus able to review their practice, make plans for the future, build team relationships, and sometimes do some trouble-shooting. Where a project staff group includes, as is usual, people from different disciplines, levels of responsibility and amounts of training, the time and cost of such an activity is more than recouped in the enhanced quality of their shared work.

Informal social contact and mutual understanding

One helpful mechanism that can serve as a counterweight to ignorance, misunderstanding and rivalry is to foster informal contact between those working with a particular problem in a given area. This might take place on neutral territory, with a chance to share lunch, exchange information about developments, and possibly have some external input so that all can learn together. Open days serve a similar purpose, dispelling myths about the setting or methods of work of others. Even a simple invitation to colleagues in other fields to make a visit can transform mutual perceptions and relationships. Knowledge and familiarity with the work of another agency make it much easier to elicit some of that agency's resources for one's clients, with the confidence that requests are likely to be appropriate. When helping clients to make an approach for a service themselves, the ability to describe what is on offer in a meaningful way is valuable. A further useful device is the provision of regularly updated information to everyone who has a particular shared concern. One excellent example is 'Meridian', compiled by the Lothian Health Promotion Department. It aims to provide information at a glance for all involved in HIV/AIDS and drugs work in Lothian. Altogether, 2500 free copies are distributed every month, which reach staff and volunteers in health, social work, community education, schools, youth work, drugs projects, self-help and voluntary groups. It includes statistics, project profiles and information about training events, books, resources of all sorts, job vacancies and new developments.

LESSONS FOR COUNSELLING IN GENERAL FROM THE COLLABORATIVE EXPERIENCE IN SOCIAL WORK

Although the task of a counselling agency is less multifaceted and less liable to misunderstanding and pressure than that of social work, some of the challenges of professional relationships are precisely the same. Just as counselling within social work is permeated by the influence of the whole inter-disciplinary and inter-agency context of the helping professions, so the specialist world of counselling cannot afford to be separated off or to function in isolation from the self-same context. It is perhaps significant that in the study by Woodhouse and Pengelly (1991), the counsellors had fewer cases including joint work with a practitioner from another agency than any other discipline. Where other workers were known to be involved with counsellors' clients, very little contact between workers was initiated from either side. This led to a degree of isolation of the counsellors, and perhaps reinforced a sense of a 'secret' relationship with the clients, In some instances, it prevented a better balance between confidentiality and cooperation being achieved.

One much neglected area of consideration in the counselling world is the extent to which the whole range of counselling skills could be of great potential value if they were explicitly seen as applicable, not only in direct client work, but also in relationships with colleagues of all sorts, both within and beyond the agency. A large share in what tends to go wrong in teams, in worker–management relationships, and in attempts to work across the boundaries of agency and profession, can be traced back to poor listening, inadequate communication, insufficient clarification of feelings and perceptions, and the lack of a supportive atmosphere to enable people to work out conflicts and attempt to change. All these are precisely the areas in which counsellors are most skilled and experienced, and yet their focus and preoccupation can sometimes seem to be directed exclusively towards their individual clients.

Counsellors and social workers appear to be located at opposite ends of the spectrum of collaborative work. Social workers, especially those in local authority departments, spend much of their time relating to others on behalf of their clients, and yet are so swamped by the pressures and demands of the external world that those transactions with others tend to be clouded by defensiveness. Counsellors have not given the whole area of shared work a great deal of explicit attention and tend to fight shy of it, so that the actual amount of contact, whether with those in other agencies, other professional disciplines, managers or policy-makers, tends to be comparatively small. There are a number of reasons for this: their narrower focus on clients' feelings and relationships, their wish to foster intimacy and privacy, their preference for leaving communication in the hands of clients, and the fact that they are not weighed down by responsibility for intervening in their clients' external world.

Significant change in both fields would therefore be beneficial. Several indicators of possible means of improving the situation, relevant to all those engaged in counselling, have emerged from this survey of the professional relationships of social workers: more inter-disciplinary training at all levels; the fostering of informal relationships at local level to allow reality-testing and greater confidence in colleagues' work; more opportunities to reflect on working relationships, perhaps with outside help; and, above all, deeper understanding of the primitive anxieties which prise people and agencies apart. But how might such steps be taken in the current political, economic and professional context? Issues like this are debated in the concluding chapter.

· SIX ·

A critique of counselling in social work

THE SOCIAL WORK PROFESSION IN DANGER

Anyone rash enough to take as a title *The Future of Social Work* invites the response that there should be a question mark after the title.

(Bamford 1990: ix)

It seems that social work has been in crisis for nearly as long as the British economy has been in decline.

(Langan 1993: 149)

The danger . . . is that social work becomes a rudderless boat being swept along by currents it knows not of, and over which it has no control.

(Lousada 1993: 105)

Statements such as these can be found in most commentaries on social work written since 1970. However, in the present climate, there is perhaps more risk to the social work profession than ever before. We need to examine in more detail the various factors contributing to such a sense of threat.

Dilemmas in professional practice

Social work faces precisely the situation so vividly described by Schön (1990) in his critique of the nature of professional practice and the dilemmas facing it. He contrasts the relatively insignificant problems it is possible to solve by means of rigorous research based on technical rationality with the confusing and ambiguous but very important human issues brought to professionals for resolution.

Describing how the latter present themselves not even as clear-cut 'problems' but as messy indeterminate situations, he catalogues their features in a way which strongly resonates with the experience of those in helping agencies. Such real-world issues tend to present themselves not as a category of problem for which a ready-made response exists, but as a series of unique cases, requiring assessment from first principles and a degree of improvisation. They usually involve a conflict of values and clash of priorities. Furthermore, there tend to be large elements of uncertainty and risk in both the situations themselves and in the interventions called for. Research findings are not experienced as sufficiently applicable in such complexity, and the conventional boundaries of professional competence no longer seem adequate to the demands of practice. In the face of these gaps between what is available and what is needed, there develops a crisis of confidence in professional practice and correspondingly in professional education.

Schön includes a whole range of professional practice – architecture, business administration, engineering, medicine and so on – in his analysis, so it is not surprising that social work, which is more subject to legislative change and media scrutiny, should experience this crisis of confidence in a most acute way. A major contributor to the problem is the fact that attacks from the outside world coincide with and amplify the serious and chronic self-doubt which exists within social work. It might be helpful at this stage to survey separately the main sources of these attacks and doubts.

External attack

A great deal has been said throughout this book about the criticism and disparagement of social work from the outside world. The strength of this cannot be adequately explained by looking merely at deliberate actions and consciously held attitudes. I believe that to understand it fully, we need to explore the powerful irrational forces at work in the environment of social work and the ways these find expression in our society's structures, institutions and attitudes. Years ago someone said that the task which society implicitly gives to social work is to 'take those we despair of, and do something with them, and no trouble please!' To the extent that social workers are identified in peoples's minds with those despaired of – 'the sad, the mad, the stupid, and the bad' – it is inevitable that these workers will share in their stigma and rejection, and be associated with those matters from which most people wish to distance themselves if they have the choice. It is not easy to be near to pain, distress and conflict, and the usual response to the threat and anxiety they represent is to put up barriers of various sorts. The siting of lunatic asylums miles from the towns is one clear historical example of this process.

A related factor in the criticism of social work is the perennial need to find someone to blame when anything goes badly wrong. The aftermath of major disasters provides a general illustration of this, as does the particular sort of witch-hunt that has followed many incidents of child abuse. While it cannot be denied that social workers and their managers made serious mistakes in some incidents, so too did many others who were not subject to the same degree of scapegoating. An unconscious yet familiar means of coping with one's own disturbing ideas and fears is to dump them on to somebody else. The paradoxical position for social work is that it serves as such a receptacle for both society's troubles and for its hopeful expectations simultaneously; *as if* it is omnipotent to solve problems and cure societal ills, and yet *as if* alone it is responsible for failing to do so. The fact that there is no consensus as to either ends or means simply increases the pressure, as does the myth that it is possible to address problems in families without some alteration in the structures in society which caused or contributed to the problem in the first place. One result of these unrealistic expectations and unfair attributions is seen in the ambivalent attitudes underpinning the extremely mixed messages given to social workers. For example, their training is regularly criticized as being too short to do justice to all that has to be learned, and yet funding to extend it to three years was denied by the self-same critics. A similar process is discernible in the way that far-reaching new statutory duties, whether in child care, mental health or care in the community, are laid on social workers at precisely the time when serious cutbacks in staffing, services and other resources are having to be made by their employers as a result of government policy on funding for both the statutory and voluntary sectors. Yet another illustration can be found in the current denial of the complexity of social problems by government ministers, who repeatedly stress that what is needed for their resolution is merely the application of basic common sense as opposed to the difficult search for agreed criteria of appropriate policies and effective methods of intervention. No wonder, therefore, in the face of all this off-loading and contradictory demand, that social work is pilloried whether it acts or refrains from action.

Internal self-doubt

These insidious processes would not have quite such a serious impact if social workers as an occupational group did not lend themselves in some way to the projections placed upon them. In any adult interaction it is rarely a case of an innocent victim and a blameworthy aggressor; far more frequently an unwitting collusion of both sides perpetuates the situation. This usually happens when external stresses are great and when historical and personality factors resonate with the particular type of anxiety involved. We therefore need to look at the specific ways social workers' own needs and expectations of themselves lead to their implicit acceptance of, and identification with, the unrealistic and unfair images placed upon them by government, media, public and employers alike.

Reference was made at the end of Chapter Three to motivation for work in the helping professions. One source of such motivation, probably quite unconscious, is an attraction to a job where the worker can cope with his or her own problems by projecting them onto others, and then have the possibility of dealing with them vicariously. So the wish to be loved and approved of, for example, or a need to take up the cudgels angrily on behalf of the underdog, could lead a worker to become over-committed and reluctant to say 'no', thereby accepting the omnipotent image. In the process, the worker is liable to stress and burn-out, and of course, failure is ultimately inevitable, so a vicious circle of low self-esteem, impaired judgement, redoubled efforts, more omnipotence and more failure is established. Such processes do not occur simply in individuals; they can be enacted collectively by whole professional groupings, and may become institutionalized in agency practices (Menzies-Lyth 1988; Woodhouse and Pengelly 1991). They can best be understood as unconscious protective mechanisms employed to ward off an intolerable level of anxiety provoked by the nature of the work.

Social workers currently suffer a chronic loss of confidence in their own value and direction. This is closely linked with the scapegoating experienced from the external world and with the tendency to collude in taking on the unreal expectations of others, and thus to become involved in the downward spiral just described. But why should they not fight back or at least defend themselves against what might with some accuracy be termed 'professional abuse'? Why has there been, on the part of professional associations and senior managers, such a silence on the subject of strengths in existing practice, and such a paucity of critical assessment of the consequences, for workers and clients alike, of new approaches such as case management? Lousada (1993) addresses this question in a way that has implications for the counselling component of social work. He sees some destructive self-criticism in operation, not only in individuals but also in the entire profession, its leaders and trainers. 'Social work's constant re-invention of itself to accommo-date the contemporary period is not a sign of flexibility but of a lack of confidence' (Lousada 1993: 104). Referring to the various fash-ions in approach which have been taken up and then discarded, much as in the counselling field, Lousada asserts that what social workers actually do best is work with individuals and families. This is partly because a particular contribution they make is to 'facilitate the *desire* for change in those whose lived experiences frequently suggest there is no hope' (ibid.: 105). And yet it is this area, the heart of social work, which is persistently attacked in an unhealthy way by the profession itself, for example by belittling such work as too 'individualistic'. The reason put forward for this seems an un-cannily close reflection of the pressures causing society's off-loading on to social work discussed earlier, namely the discomfort and ambivalence which results from being too close to the damage suf-fered by clients. But surely, one may argue, this is precisely what social workers have chosen to be employed to do! This is indeed the case, and until relatively recently the extent of client distress has not prevented them from doing a reasonably good job with some pride. It would appear, therefore, that other factors are intervening to disturb the balance and to throw social work off course. We do not need to look far to discover at least some of the culprits: one is the weight of derogatory attitudes from the outside world already dis-cussed, another is the fact that the provision of appropriate support and supervision is not keeping pace with an increasingly difficult workload, and yet another is the massive impingement of com-munity care thinking and new forms of practice associated with it. These two final points need to be spelt out in more detail.

STRESS, SUPPORT AND PROFESSIONAL DEVELOPMENT

It is important to look further at the nature and source of stresses encountered in helping work. Some of these are common to both counselling and social work, for example the pervasiveness of 'loss' in the problems dealt with, while other stresses may belong pre-dominantly to one or the other type of work, for example the particular case of violence as it affects social workers. Understand-ing in more depth how difficult it is to cope constructively with such upsetting and deeply anxiety-provoking issues may give some indication of the reasons for the current high incidence of stress-related illness and behaviour in those in the front line of caring, and of the support and learning which is needed to maintain an effective level of work and morale.

Loss

Counsellors and social workers have in common the fact that a very large proportion of the difficulties brought to them by clients is related to serious loss. It is well-known that bereavement can give rise to many other problems such as mental or physical ill health, poverty, marital and family conflict, poor functioning at school or work, and social isolation, any of which may bring someone to seek help. Less evident perhaps, but equally significant, is the deleterious impact of other types of loss on people's security and sense of identity. Examples include the experience of redundancy, the birth of a handicapped child, desertion by an attachment figure, the diagnosis of a life-threatening illness, the need of an elderly person to enter residential care, or indeed any major life change. Anxiety is a predominant emotion as people go through a crisis of disorientation and struggle to find continuity and meaning in their experience. This is true of any loss, but the problems are compounded when, for example, a major disaster occurs, or when children have to cope with the the death of a parent from AIDS. To remain sensitively on the receiving end of all the intense and mixed feelings brought about by human tragedy, workers require not only the right personality and training, but also a range of adequate support systems. Good staff supervision, as discussed in Chapter Four, is a major contributor to responsive work. Consultancy is sometimes valuable, especially at times of reorganization (which brings about change and loss for the workers themselves) or when conflict and tension are militating against the full use of workers' skills. Illustrations of this were offered in Chapter Five. Peer support, regular in-service training, enabling management and ongoing personal learning are also vital, and yet, paradoxically, these are precisely the things which become more scarce as pressures increase.

Violence towards social workers

Some of social work's concerns are not the ones with which most counsellors can currently closely identify. Violence towards social workers provides a good example. By the late 1980s, several social workers had died at the hands of their clients. The risks faced by

social workers thus came into sharp focus and led to the recognition
of the disturbingly large scale of the problem:

> [Social workers] are verbally abused, suffer damage to their
> property, . . . have been beaten up, . . . held hostage and men-
> aced with weapons, . . . seriously injured in assaults with deadly
> weapons, and in car accidents caused by clients. They have
> been blinded in acid attacks, sexually assaulted, raped and
> murdered.
>
> (BASW 1988: 2–3)

Workers are likely to be emotionally as well as physically damaged by such experiences, especially if the responses of colleagues,
managers, employers and the general public are inadequate and
unsympathetic. More rigorous attempts are now being made to
offer guidelines for prevention where possible, for coping with violence when it occurs, and for better management and help with its
after-effects. The high incidence of violence is a measure of the
degree of dangerousness with which social workers have to deal.
Among the most risky situations are work in residential and day
care, visits to clients in their own homes, work affecting the liberty
of a client, court appearances, case reviews and having to refuse
services. The workload of most social workers includes at least
some of these situations, all of which have a significant counselling
component requiring well-developed skills. The extra dimensions
of self-awareness, knowledge, teamwork and good communication
needed for effective assessment and management of risk are only
now beginning to be fully appreciated. Since unhappily there is an
upsurge of violence in society generally, it may not be long before
counsellors in other contexts have to face similar risky encounters.
Some of the discussions and guidelines produced by social workers
(Brown *et al.* 1986; Strathclyde Regional Council 1987; BASW
1988) may be found useful more generally.

MANAGERIALISM AND THE PRESSURE OF
MARKET FORCES

The advent of the ideology of community care poses a particularly
significant culture shift for social work, to the extent that it has
been described as a revolution. Because it is one expression of the
prevailing ethos contained in one piece of recent government legislation after another, not only social work but also health, education and other institutions in society are experiencing a similar

massive impact. A most powerful and pervasive influence is the new public management thinking, with its emphasis less on policy than on a contractual approach, competitive tenders, cost-effectiveness, output targets, performance appraisal and so on. Such ideas from the world of business, with their accompanying new vocabulary – case management, purchasers and providers, consumers, packages of care – seem quite alien to the values of caring and can with some justification be seen as a fundamental attack on them. The great challenge now having to be faced, therefore, is to find ways of coming to terms with this emerging business culture without allowing these core social work values to be jeopardized. Because the attack seems to be targetted particularly on work with the most vulnerable members of the community, and on approaches mediated in large degree through personal relationships, it is the counselling dimensions of the social work task which are especially threatened. A look at the scale of counselling in social work will give an indication of the seriousness of the problem.

THE EXTENT OF THE COUNSELLING TASK IN SOCIAL WORK

Various attempts have been made to categorize the various groups of workers whose jobs include counselling. Woolfe *et al.* (1989) first separate out those whose primary professional training is in counselling, subdividing this group into people employed full-time as counsellors and those who practise in a largely voluntary capacity. People whose primary professional training is not in counselling (e.g. psychologists, nurses, social workers) are similarly subdivided into those employed full-time as counsellors and others not so employed though using counselling skills in their work. A final category identifies those more committed to community self-help than to counselling, who offer support, befriending, advocacy, information and so on. This admittedly tentative framework is useful in providing a degree of structure or shape to a scene which can seem extremely amorphous and chaotic. However, an attempt to place social work practice accurately within these categories highlights a real gap, an area of counselling practice hitherto scarcely acknowledged.

A significant proportion of social workers have job descriptions which explicitly give a high profile to counselling as such. On the other hand, in mainstream social work, counselling is rarely a separate entity offered explicitly in its own right. However, just because counselling is not rigidly demarcated from the other aspects of social work practice does not mean that it is non-existent. Most commonly it is a highly significant component of the work, a fact which is often overlooked or misunderstood. The confusion arises when a simplistic distinction is drawn between 'full-time employment as a counsellor' on the one hand, and 'counselling skills as an adjunct to helping work' underpinning other types of activity on the other. This dichotomy allows for no middle ground, and yet I am convinced that it is in the space between these two entities that a great deal of actual practice in social work takes place. As we saw in Chapter Two, the Barclay Report identified counselling as one of the two main activities of social workers, the other being social care planning, and the report acknowledged the interlocking nature of these activities. The particular, perhaps unique, challenge faced by social workers is to offer counselling in a way that is integrated appropriately with a variety of other approaches in the overall work with a given client, often within the same interview.

A logical categorization of the counselling dimensions of social work would therefore be as follows:

- counselling skills underpinning the whole range of social work tasks;
- counselling as a significant component of the work, carried out in conjunction with other approaches;
- counselling as a major explicit part of the job description.

Each of these requires discussion in its own right.

Counselling skills underpinning social work tasks

There is no dispute that the entire range of social work activity, in whatever setting, requires a sound underpinning of the approaches and skills now generally understood as 'counselling skills'. This is as true for activities like community work or welfare rights, whose practitioners are less closely identified with counselling, as it is for residential and day care, group work and interventions with families. As Bamford (1989: 138) says:

> The core of social work remains the relationship between worker and client . . . the attitudes shown by the social worker remain critical determinants of the service offered. Warmth, openness and respect shown by the worker can, at the lowest, provide clients with an experience of public bureaucracies different in character from that usually experienced . . . Allied to effective

intervention, those qualities can on occasion have a significant impact on the life of the client.

Counselling as a significant function carried out in conjunction with other approaches

This category includes perhaps the majority of social workers based in local authority area teams. They are the ones whose work has a large statutory component: report-writing, information-sharing with other agencies, an element of 'social policing', home-visiting, resource mobilization and advocacy are typical tasks. The impact of various role conflicts on social workers was explored in Chapter Three; these are particularly relevant for workers in this category. It is important not to underestimate the way in which such conflicts and tensions between different aspects of the task can affect and sometimes militate against the counselling component of the work. However, their existence does not automatically imply that counselling cannot be done. The real question is the extent to which the challenges can be faced and the obstacles surmounted.

A client approaching a counselling agency is normally aware that a particular type of approach is the one on offer, a service described as 'counselling', however that activity is initially understood. By contrast, in social work, although self-referrals constitute a significant proportion of all requests for help, most of these are not for 'counselling' as such, but for some practical service or piece of advice or, even more often, because of some undefined malaise or difficulty in functioning. Many of the referrals made to social workers by others on behalf of a client are described in behavioural terms, for example when it becomes apparent that someone is failing to cope with some aspect of their lives in a sufficiently serious way to cause concern to others. The actual means of addressing this situation is left to the worker to assess through developing a relationship with the client and negotiating at least an implicit contract.

A friend in the counselling field objected to my view that social workers in this intermediate position are providing legitimate counselling. This objection was made on the grounds that the client may well not have been *explicitly* offered counselling, and this term 'explicitly' is, in the eyes of the British Association for Counselling, 'the dividing line between the counselling task and *ad hoc* counselling, and is the major safeguard of the rights of the consumer' (BAC 1985: 2). In an interesting comment on these issues, Woolfe *et al.* (1989) support the notion of a continuum rather than two polarities and acknowledge that neat and tidy definitions may not fit the complexity and messiness of the real world, and yet conclude that the BAC definition is something to which all people practising counselling skills should seek to aspire. However, when we look closer at what it is that is to be offered, we see that it is *'time, attention and respect* to ... persons temporarily in the role of client' (BAC 1985: 1; emphasis added), a situation which accurately describes social work activity.

It is important, however, to take any reservations seriously, especially when questions about safeguarding the rights of the consumer are being raised. Possibly the thorniest problem arises where there are restrictions on the client's freedom to accept or reject what is being offered. Many social work clients are subject to experiences of compulsion; a report is required by the court, a person may be detained in hospital under the Mental Health Act, a child may be taken to a place of safety, and an elderly person at risk may have no choice but to 'accept' residential care. Of course, the action taken when it comes to the crunch will need to be underpinned by counselling skills if the client's dignity and remaining areas of discretion are to be preserved. But, in addition, and most importantly, these are all situations which have precursors and aftermaths, during which the relationship with the worker and the counselling activity undertaken will make a very significant difference to the overall outcome of the intervention. Calming someone beset by panic or anger, eliciting a modicum of cooperation from a distrustful and resistant client, helping some unpalatable realities to be confronted, appreciating some of the reasons for primitive emotions and facilitating the expression of contradictory feelings, are all extremely skilled counselling tasks, made very much more difficult by the harsh unpromising circumstances in which they have to be attempted. This is a far cry from the security and relative tranquillity of a consulting room session with a highly motivated, cooperative client.

Counselling as a major explicit part of the job description

Many social workers employed in voluntary organizations and specialist projects, or working in hospitals, clinics, schools and general practice, fall into this category. Their formal title is unlikely to include the word 'counsellor', although in their job description counselling is in most cases given a great deal of emphasis. Their way of working is practically indistinguishable from, or at least overlaps to a great extent with, that of a 'counsellor' or anyone from a different profession in a largely counselling role. Activities of a social worker attached to general practice, for example, will probably include work in terminal care and bereavement counselling, thinking through with a family the implications of the birth of a handicapped child, helping someone to decide about abortion or an HIV test, supporting a family caring for an elderly dependant relative, liaising with social workers based elsewhere, and linking the practice with relevant resources in the local community. Many of these workers develop specialist expertise, whether in a specific problem area such as alcohol and drug abuse, or a developmental phase like adolescence or old age, or an area of responsibility like adoption and fostering, or a particular approach such as crisis intervention. They are therefore often used as resource people and consulted by social workers carrying a more wide-ranging caseload.

There are factors militating against the full exploitation of all the potential which clearly exists when social workers are able to function largely in acknowledged counselling roles. Economic constraints, the fortress mentality brought about by media criticism and unrealistic expectations, and perhaps especially the priority allocated to statutory involvement, all mean that fewer social workers than previously are free to engage in preventive and therapeutic initiatives, and find themselves having to respond reactively to 'at risk' situations. In common with professionals in other fields, such as psychologists in health or education, they are now also having to make a case for intensive longer-term work to those preoccupied more by rapid turnover, impressive statistics and budgetary control than by the painstaking effort required to mitigate fundamental human problems.

RELATIONSHIPS BETWEEN COUNSELLING AND SOCIAL WORK

Divisive factors

Ignorance and misunderstanding about the nature of social work and counselling can be attributed not only to outsiders, but also to practitioners in each field; myths and stereotypes abound to such an extent that mutual disparagement is often encountered. The danger is that a sharp polarization between counsellors and social workers becomes established, which then damages their relationships with each other and gives a misleading impression of their work to outsiders. The nature of this polarization is tellingly captured in a comment made sixty years ago: 'Doing case work seems to

some like setting out deck chairs for the comfort of a few passengers
when everyone on board a sinking ship should be manning the life
boats' (Reynolds 1934: 125). The split in attributions and perceptions, only slightly caricatured, is of counselling being 'precious'
and over-protected, even a fashionable activity of articulate middle-
class people with time and money, while social work has to cope
with being the 'dustbin' of society's problems, identified with the
marginalized and deprived segments of the population. This split
has been reinforced in various ways. A contribution to the rift is
made when some counsellors collude with the myth that social
workers are universal providers by sending along their most diffi-
cult-to-help clients, often without any prior discussion as to what
might be achieved. Another is that 'counselling' has tended to
become a catchword, carelessly used to refer to other quite different
activities, such as 'beauty counselling' or 'business counselling', thus
either devaluing its currency or confusing counselling with advice-
giving. A further divisive factor is a sense of exclusivity conveyed,
perhaps unwittingly, by BAC's extremely stringent accreditation
arrangements, valuable and essential as these are to establishing
the credibility of the embryonic counselling profession. The fact
that both fields are subject to rapid change, and therefore to a lot
of turbulence, means that both are suffering transitional stress
and are being required to make adaptations experienced as more
painful than helpful. At such times, it is harder than ever to
establish good communication based on accurate perceptions. The
cumulative result of these attitudes and trends is that mutual relationships almost inevitably suffer. In all stereotyping activity, sub-
tleties are overlooked and the real nature of both activities becomes
obscured. Another casualty of this process is mutual awareness
of their common ground, including shared areas of concern, overlapping approaches and potential to complement each other.

Unifying tendencies

Counselling and social work share many fundamental aims and
values. In one of the rare contemporary discussions of 'casework',
Doyle (1994), having described its long and honourable history,
goes on to reiterate its underpinning principles in terms of the
consistent value placed on the individual, a basic respect which
transcends a person's role, status or behaviour, acceptance and the
right to expression of feelings. She believes it is imperative that
social work must continue to demand such attitudes and rights for
all, as the only way to protect the most vulnerable from oppression,

and to avoid labelling people as 'undeserving'. It seems unlikely that counsellors would disagree with this.

It is perhaps a measure of the common ground between counselling and social work in terms of overlapping approaches and methods that a great deal of the literature in one field has much relevance for work in the other. For example, apart from their particular application to a given context, many social work texts focusing on skills are practically indistinguishable from, and could easily serve as, counselling texts, despite the fact that they may never mention the word 'counselling'. A case in point is Lishman's (1994) *Communication in Social Work*, which clearly and thoroughly addresses topics like symbolic, verbal and non-verbal communication, the qualities needed to build and maintain client–worker relationships, ways of attending and listening, the use of contracts, and ways of intervening to change attitudes and behaviour. All this is informed by thought-provoking research into client perceptions of the help they felt they had received. The extent to which practitioners do in fact draw upon each other's writings is not certain; ignorance about what is on offer, a tendency to be insular and inward-looking, and the prejudices just discussed all militate against optimum cross-fertilization of this sort, which is a great pity. One positive development is that there are now more books which span various fields of helping work without being labelled as belonging too narrowly to only one segment. A good example is *Supervision in the Helping Professions* by Hawkins and Shohet (1989).

Encounters in training can establish accurate mutual understanding. A significant number of people may have dual training, for example in social work followed or preceded by counselling. Many students on substantial counselling courses are in this position; some of them find employment as 'counsellors', whereas others remain in their existing posts practising counselling to a greater and much better informed extent than previously, and enabling colleagues in their own profession to have a better grasp of the nature of counselling and what it might offer. At present, such connections happen by chance; so far there have been few deliberate attempts to forge closer training links, although, as discussed in Chapter Five, this idea has potential.

Mutual learning from each other's particular strengths

The degree of common cause just outlined does give grounds for some optimism about the possibilites of bridge-building. It is not at all surprising, given the different influences and pressures on each sphere of activity, that their development has been uneven and that contrasting patterns of strengths and weaknesses have emerged, some of which have pushed the two activities apart. It is important, therefore, to try to identify some of the positive learning from each field which could benefit the other.

Social work has done a great deal of thinking, experimenting and writing about *practice teaching of students*. As described in Chapter Four, there has been some identification of what makes for positive professional placement learning for students, and of ways of preparing practitioners for this crucial task, and the processes of student supervision have been conceptualized. The fruits of this could readily be applied to all forms of counselling.

Social work has also taken on board the whole issue of *anti-discriminatory practice* in its various forms, and in particular has tried very hard to find ways of integrating anti-racist and ethnically sensitive practice into social work education. The fact that this is proving to be a contentious and often painful process, provoking highly ambivalent reactions from government and the media, is in itself symptomatic evidence of the very problem it is attempting to address. This makes it even more important that counselling practitioners consolidate and develop their own stance on the matter. Perhaps they could join forces with social workers in combatting the worst forms of institutionalized prejudice on behalf of their clients.

The higher priority given by counsellors to the *development of self-awareness* is something they could offer to social work. The more damaged and disturbed the client group is, the greater is the need for self-knowledge on the part of the worker, in order to avoid being sucked into collusion, retaliatory behaviour or unhelpful distancing. Counselling training has grasped this particular nettle much more than social work.

Equally, social workers could learn a lot from counsellors' relatively single-minded focus on the *interactions of client and worker in an actual session*. This would serve as a useful antidote to their preoccupation with so many diverse and distracting demands for their attention, helping them to reflect in more depth on the meaning of clients' behaviour and to make more sense of their often confusing and contradictory communications. Psychodynamic concepts of counter-transference and projective identification have relevance here for both counsellors and social workers, as they provide a valuable insight into ways of using the intense feelings stirred up in the worker by the client's story to illuminate the client's underlying problem (Temperley 1979; Brearley 1991).

In order to ensure their *survival*, many counselling agencies and training institutions have long experience in making a case for their existence to funding bodies. They, like social work, are now having to live in a much harsher economic, political and philosophical climate, which tends to downgrade and devalue their work. Again, shared thinking at various levels might help each grouping to feel stronger and less isolated.

CONCLUSION

I have attempted to make clear that what above all is required of social workers is that they effectively offer help with people's subjective feelings, private troubles and disrupted relationships (the traditional concern of social casework and more recently of counselling), while simultaneously fulfilling an extensive range of statutory requirements in relation to some of the most vulnerable people in our society. Because they are given authority to use scarce public resources, it is inevitable that social workers get swept up in the contentious politics of social provision. Where other forms of helping provision can remain relatively invisible, social work is in the unenviable position of being closely scrutinized by the media, and used as a scapegoat when things go wrong. The role conflicts they experience, the frequent changes in social policy and legislation, the cutbacks in resources, and the impossible expectations placed on them, taken together, are undermining confidence and hence their professional competence. The irony is that skills in counselling are required in social work to a greater extent than ever before, and yet the means of developing and using them has never been more threatened.

If the best of the legacy of social work's long history, coupled with all the potential of an in-depth understanding of counselling, were fully appreciated, the wisdom they offer could be extremely fruitfully applied to all aspects of helping work, not just that concerned with direct face-to-face involvement with clients. Counselling insights are also invaluable in relations with colleagues. Why should they not be used in staff groups and with those in other disciplines and agencies? Could they not have a higher profile in training? It is likely that if the self-same communication skills that counsellors and social workers aim to use in dealings with their clients were also employed in their transactions with those in the outside world, such as policy makers, managers and funders, then the gulf of misunderstanding and disparagement of human values of caring, which is becoming ever more serious, might be diminished. If this proves impossible, then the future welfare of service-users of all sorts is bleak indeed.

References

Ahmad, B. (1990) *Black Perspectives in Social Work*. Birmingham: BASW/ Venture Press.

Ahmed, S., Cheetham, J. and Small, J. (eds) (1987) *Social Work with Black Children and their Families*. London: Batsford/BAAF.

Ambrose, A. (1989) Key concepts of the transitional approach to managing change, in L. Klein (ed.), *Working with Organisations*. London: Tavistock Institute of Human Relations.

Archer, L. and Whitaker, D. (1992) Decisions, tasks and uncertainties in child protection work, *Journal of Social Work Practice*, 6(1): 63–75.

Bacon, R. (1988) Counter-transference in a case conference: Resistance and rejection in work with abusing families and their children, in G. Pearson, J. Treseder and M. Yelloly (eds), *Social Work and the Legacy of Freud: Psychoanalysis and Its Uses*. Basingstoke: Macmillan Educational.

Bailey, R. and Brake, M. (eds) (1975) *Radical Social Work*. London: Edward Arnold.

Balint, M. (1964) *The Doctor, His Patient and the Illness*. Tunbridge Wells: Pitman Medical.

Bamford, T. (1989) Discretion and Managerialism, in S. Shardlow (ed.) *The Values of Change in Social Work*. London: Tavistock/Routledge.

Bamford, T. (1990) *The Future of Social Work*. Basingstoke: Macmillan.

Bang, S. (1983) *We Come as a Friend: Towards a Vietnamese Model of Social Work*. Derby: Refugee Action.

Barclay, P. (1982) *Social Workers: Their Role and Tasks*. London: Bedford Square Press.

Bar-On, A. (1990) Organisational resource mobilisation: A hidden face of social work practice, *British Journal of Social Work*, 20: 133–49.

Beckford Report (1985) *A Child in Trust*. London: London Borough of Brent.

Berry, J. (1971) Helping children directly, *British Journal of Social Work*, 1(3): 315–32.

Biestek, F. (1961) *The Casework Relationship*. London: Allen and Unwin.

Biggs, S. (1991) Community care, case management and the psychodynamic perspective, *Journal of Social Work Practice*, 5(1): 71–81.

Birch Report (1976) *Working Party on Manpower and Training for the Social Services*. London: HMSO.

Blech, G. (1981) How to prevent 'burn out' of social workers, in S. Martel (ed.), *Supervision and Team Support*. London: Family Service Units/Bedford Square Press.

Bloch, S. (1982) *What is Psychotherapy?* Oxford: Oxford University Press.

Brearley, J. (1989) Anxiety and its management in health care: Implications for social work, in R. Taylor and J. Ford (eds), *Social Work and Health Care*. Research Highlights in Social Work No. 19. London: Jessica Kingsley.

Brearley, J. (1991) A psychodynamic approach to social work, in J. Lishman (ed.) *Handbook of Theory for Practice Teachers in Social Work*. London: Jessica Kingsley.

Brearley, J. (1992) Community and organisation: Managing the boundaries at a time of change, in S. Baron and J.D. Haldane (eds), *Community, Normality and Difference: Meeting Special Needs*. Aberdeen: Aberdeen University Press.

Brearley, M. (1986) Counsellors and clients: Men or women?, *Marriage Guidance*, 22(2): 2–9.

Bridger, H. (1981) *Consultative Work with Communities and Organisations: Towards a Psychodynamic Image of Man*. Malcolm Miller Lecture. Aberdeen: Aberdeen University Press.

British Association for Counselling (1984) *Code of Ethics and Practice for Counsellors*. Rugby: BAC.

British Association for Counselling (1985) *Counselling: Definition of Terms in Use, with Expansion and Rationale*. Rugby: BAC.

British Association of Social Workers (1975) *A Code of Ethics for Social Workers*. Birmingham: BASW Publications.

British Association of Social Workers (1977) *The Social Work Task*. Birmingham: BASW Publications.

British Association of Social Workers (1988) *Violence to Social Workers*. Birmingham: BASW Publications.

Brown, D. and Pedder, J. (1991) *Introduction to Psychotherapy: An Outline of Psychodynamic Principles and Practice*, 2nd edn. London: Routledge.

Brown, H. and Pearce, J. (1992) Good practice in the face of anxiety: Social work with girls and young women, *Journal of Social Work Practice*, 6(2): 159–66.

Brown, R., Bute, S. and Ford, P. (1986) *Social Workers at Risk*. Basingstoke: Macmillan.

Burgess, H. and Jackson, S. (1990) Enquiry and action learning – a new approach to social work education, *Social Work Education*, 9(3): 1–17.

Burnham, J. (1986) *Family Therapy*. London: Routledge.

Butler-Sloss, E. (1988) *Report of the Inquiry into Child Abuse in Cleveland 1987*. Cmnd 412. London: HMSO.

Butrym, Z. (1976) *The Nature of Social Work*. Basingstoke: Macmillan.

Carlile Report (1987) *A Child in Mind: Protection of Children in a Responsible Society*. London: London Borough of Greenwich.

Carmichael, K. (1991) *Ceremony of Innocence: Tears, Power and Protest*. Basingstoke: Macmillan.

Cawley, R. (1977) The teaching of psychotherapy, *Association of University Teachers of Psychiatry Newsletter*, (January 1977) 19–36.

Central Council for Education and Training in Social Work (1991) *Rules and Requirements for the Diploma in Social Work*. CCETSW Paper No. 30. London: CCETSW.

Charles-Edwards, D. (1988) Counselling, management and BAC, *Counselling*, 63: 10.

Charles-Edwards, D., Dryden, W. and Woolfe, R. Professional issues in Counselling, in W. Dryden et al. (eds) (1989) *Handbook of Counselling in Britain*. London: Routledge.

Clarke, J. (ed.) (1993) *A Crisis in Care? Challenges to Social Work*. London: Sage/Open University.

Collins English Dictionary (1991). 3rd Edition. Glasgow: HarperCollins.

Colman, W. (1989) *On Call: The Work of a Telephone Helpline for Child Abusers*. Aberdeen: Aberdeen University Press.

Conn, J. (1993) Delicate liaisons: The impact of gender differences on the supervisory relationship within social services, *Journal of Social Work Practice*, 7(1): 41–53.

Corney, R. and Jenkins, R. (1993) *Counselling in General Practice*. London: Tavistock/Routledge.

Corrigan, P. and Leonard, P. (1978) *Social Work Practice under Capitalism: A Marxist Approach*. London: Macmillan.

Coulshed, V. (1990) *Management in Social Work*. London: Macmillan/BASW.

Coulshed, V. (1991) *Social Work Practice: An Introduction*, 2nd edn. Basingstoke: Macmillan.

Croft, S. and Beresford, P. (1994) A participatory approach to social work, in C. Hanvey and T. Philpot (eds), *Practising Social Work*. London: Routledge.

d'Ardenne, P. and Mahtani, A. (1989) *Transcultural Counselling in Action*. London: Sage.

Dearnley, B. (1985) A plain man's guide to supervision – or new clothes for the emperor?, *Journal of Social Work Practice*, 2(1): 52–65.

Deed, D. (1962) Danger of stereotypes in student supervision, *Case Conference*, 9: 1.

Department of Health and Social Security (1974) *Report of Committee of Inquiry into the Care and Supervision Provided in Relation to Maria Colwell*. London: HMSO.

Department of Health and Social Security (1978) *Social Service Teams: The Practitioner's View*. London: HMSO.

Department of Health and Social Security (1985) *Child Abuse Inquiries*. London: HMSO.

Department of Health (1989) *Caring for People: Community Care in the Next Decade and Beyond*, Cm. 849. London: HMSO.

Department of Health (1991) *Child Abuse: A Study of Inquiry Reports 1980–1989*. London: HMSO.

Doel, M. and Lawson, B. (1986) Open records: The client's right to partnership, *British Journal of Social Work*, 16: 407–30.

Dominelli, L. (1988) *Anti-Racist Social Work*. Basingstoke: Macmillan.

Downie, R.S. and Telfer, E. (1969) *Respect for Persons*. London: Allen and Unwin.

Doyle, C. (1994) Casework, in C. Hanvey and T. Philpot (eds), *Practising Social Work*. London: Routledge.

Dryden, W. and Thorne, B. (eds) (1991) *Training and Supervision for Counselling in Action*. London: Sage.

Dryden, W., Charles-Edwards, D. and Woolfe, R. (eds) (1989) *Handbook of Counselling in Britain*. London: Routledge.

Emery, F. (ed.) (1969) *Systems Thinking*. London: Penguin.

Finch, J. and Groves, D. (eds) (1983) *A Labour of Love: Women, Work and Caring*. London: Routledge and Kegan Paul.

Forster, J. (1988) *Divorce Advice and Counselling for Men*. Edinburgh: Scottish Marriage Guidance Council.

France, A. (1988) *Consuming Psychotherapy*. London: Free Association Books.

Gardiner, D. (1989) *The Anatomy of Supervision: Developing Learning and Professional Competence for Social Work Students*. Milton Keynes: Society for Research in Higher Education/Open University Press.

Garrett, A. (1954) Learning through supervision, *Smith College Studies in Social Work*, 24: 2.

Goldstein, H. (1973) *Social Work Practice: A Unitary Approach*. Columbia, SC: University of South Carolina Press.

Griffiths, R. (1988) *Community Care: Agenda for Action*. London: HMSO.

Hall, S. (1980) Race, articulation and societies structured in dominance, in UNESCO (ed.) *Sociological Theories: Race and Colonialism*, 304–5.

Hallett, C. (1989) Child-abuse inquiries and public policy, in O. Stevenson (ed.), *Child Abuse*. Hemel Hempstead: Harvester Wheatsheaf.

Halmos, P. (1965) *The Faith of the Counsellors*. London: Constable.

Hanmer, J. and Statham, D. (1988) *Women and Social Work: Towards a Woman-Centred Practice*. Basingstoke: Macmillan Educational.

Hawkins, P. and Shohet, R. (1989) *Supervision in the Helping Professions*. Milton Keynes: Open University Press.

Heywood, J. (1964) *An Introduction to Teaching Casework Skills*. London: Routledge and Kegan Paul.

Hillman, J. and Mackenzie, M. (1993) *Understanding Field Social Work*. Birmingham: BASW/Venture Press.

Hollis, F. (1964) *Casework: A Psychosocial Therapy*, New York: Random House.

Hooper, D. and Dryden, W. (1991) *Couple Therapy*. Buckingham: Open University Press.

Hornby, S. (1993) *Collaborative Care: Interprofessional, Interagency and Interpersonal*. Oxford: Blackwell.

Howe, D. (1993) *On Being a Client: Understanding the Process of Counselling and Psychotherapy*. London: Sage.

Humphries, B. *et al.* (1993) *Improving Practice Teaching and Learning*. London: CCETSW.

Institute of Almoners (1953) Report of the survey committee, *The Almoner*, 6(2): 61–9.

Jacobs, M. (1988) *Psychodynamic Counselling in Action*. London: Sage.

Jordan, B. (1984) *Invitation to Social Work*. Oxford: Martin Robertson.

Jordan, B. (1990) *Social Work in an Unjust Society*. Hemel Hempstead: Harvester Wheatsheaf.

Kadushin, A. (1976) *Supervision in Social Work*. New York: Columbia University Press.

Kahn, J. and Earle, E. (1982) *The Cry for Help and the Professional Response*. Oxford: Pergamon Press.

Kareem, J. (1978) Conflicting concepts of mental health in a multi-cultural society, *Psychiatrica Clinica*, 11: 90–95.

Kilbrandon Report (1964) *Report of the Committee on Children and Young Persons (Scotland)*. Cmnd 2306. Edinburgh: HMSO.

King, M. and Trowell, J. (1992) *Children's Welfare and the Law: The Limits of Legal Intervention*. London: Sage.

Kwhali, J. (1991) Assessment checklists for DipSW external assessors, in *One Small Step towards Racial Justice: The Teaching of Antiracism in Diploma in Social Work Programmes*. London: CCETSW.

Langan, M. (1993) The rise and fall of social work, in J. Clarke (ed.), *A Crisis in Care: Challenges to Social Work*. London: Sage/Open University.

Lishman, J. (1994) *Communication in Social Work*. Basingstoke: Macmillan.

Lorde, A. (1984) *Sister Outsider*. New York: The Crossing Press.

Lousada, J. (1993) Self-defence is no offence, *Journal of Social Work Practice*, 7(2): 103–113.

McBoyle Report (1963) *Report of the Committee on the Prevention of Neglect of Children*. Edinburgh: HMSO.

Mattinson, J. (1975) *The Reflection Process in Casework Supervision*. London: Institute of Marital Studies/Tavistock Institute of Human Relations.

Mattinson, J. and Sinclair, I. (1979) *Mate and Stalemate*. Oxford: Blackwell.

Menzies-Lyth, I. (1988) *Containing Anxiety in Institutions: Selected Essays*. London: Free Association Books.

Menzies-Lyth, I. (1989) *The Dynamics of the Social: Selected Essays*. London: Free Association Books.

Morgan, G. (1986) *Images of Organization*. Beverly Hills, CA: Sage.

Nicholas, J. (1992) The inside story: On seeing clients in their own homes, in E. Noonan and L. Spurling (eds), *The Making of a Counsellor*. London: Routledge.

Noonan, E. (1983) *Counselling Young People*. London: Methuen.

Oatley, K. (1984) *Selves in Relation: An Introduction to Psychotherapy Groups*. London: Methuen.

Øvretveit, J. (1993) *Coordinating Community Care: Multidisciplinary Teams and Care Management*. Buckingham: Open University Press.

Parton, C. and Parton, N. (1989) Child protection: The law and dangerousness, in O. Stevenson (ed.), *Child Abuse*. Hemel Hempstead: Harvester Wheatsheaf.

Payne, M. (1985) The code of ethics, the social work manager and the organisation, in D. Watson (ed.), *A Code of Ethics for Social Work: The Second Step*. London: Routledge and Kegan Paul.

Pearson, G., Treseder, J. and Yelloly, M. (eds) (1988) *Social Work and the Legacy of Freud: Psychoanalysis and Its Uses*. Basingstoke: Macmillan Educational.

Perlman, H. (1957) Social casework in social work: Its place and purpose, in G. Parker, (ed.), *Casework within Social Work*, 2nd edn. Newcastle upon Tyne: Department of Social Studies, University of Newcastle upon Tyne.

Phillipson, J. (1992) *Practising Equality: Women, Men and Social Work*. London: CCETSW.

Pincus, A. and Minahan, A. (1973) *Social Work Practice: Model and Method*. Itasca, IL: Peacock.

Preston-Shoot, M. and Agass, D. (1990) *Making Sense of Social Work: Psychodynamics, Systems and Practice*. Basingstoke: Macmillan Educational.

Reynolds, B. (1934) Between client and community: A study of responsibility in social casework, *Smith College Studies in Social Work*, 5(1): 125.

Richmond, M. (1917) *Social Diagnosis*. New York: Russell Sage.

Rosenblatt, A. and Mayer, J. (1975) Objectionable supervisory styles: students' views, *Social Work (U.S.A.)*, 20(3): 184–9.

Satyamurti, C. (1981) *Occupational Survival*. Oxford: Blackwell.

Scarman Report (1981) The Brixton Disorders. London: HMSO.

Schön, D. (1990) *Educating the Reflective Practitioner*. Bristol: Jossey-Bass.

Secker, J. (1993) *From Theory to Practice in Social Work: The Development of Social Work Students' Practice*. Aldershot: Avebury.

Seebohm Report (1968) *Report of the Committee on Local Authority and Allied Personal Social Services*. Cmnd 3703. London: HMSO.

Shardlow, S. (1989) *The Values of Change in Social Work*. London: Tavistock/ Routledge.

Skynner, R. (1976) *One Flesh: Separate Persons*. London: Constable.

Skynner, R. (1989) Make sure to feed the goose that lays the golden eggs: A discussion on the myth of altruism, in J. Schlapobersky (ed.), *Institutes and How to Survive Them*. London: Methuen.

Specht, H. and Vickery, A. (eds) (1977) *Integrating Social Work Methods*. London: Allen and Unwin.

Stainton Rogers, W. *et al.* (1989) *Child Abuse and Neglect*. London: The Open University/Batsford.

Storrie, J. (1992) Mastering interprofessionalism – an enquiry into the development of master programmes with an interprofessional focus, *Journal of Interprofessional Care*, 6(3), 253–60.

Strathclyde Regional Council, Social Work Department (1987) *Violence to Staff: Policies and Procedures*. Glasgow: Strathclyde Regional Council.

Sutherland, J.D. (ed.) (1971) *Towards Community Mental Health*. London: Tavistock.

Temperley, J. (1979) The implications for social work practice of recent psychoanalytical developments, in *Change and Renewal in Psychodynamic Social Work*. Oxford: Smith College School for Social Work/Group for Advancement of Psychotherapy in Social Work.

Timms, N. (1970) *Social Work: An Outline for the Intending Student*. London: Routledge and Kegan Paul.

Timms, N. (1989) Social work values: Context and contribution, in S. Shardlow (ed.), *The Values of Change in Social Work*. London: Tavistock/Routledge.

Towle, C. (1954) *The Learner in Education for the Professions as seen in Education for Social Work*. Chicago, IL: University of Chicago Press.

Treacher, A. and Carpenter, J. (eds) (1984) *Using Family Therapy*. Oxford: Blackwell.

Triseliotis, J. (1986) Transcultural social work, in J. Cox (ed.), *Transcultural Psychiatry*. London: Croom Helm.

Trist, E. and Murray H. (eds) (1990) *The Social Engagement of Social Science, Vol. 1: The Socio-Psychological Perspective*. Philadelphia, PA: University of Pennsylvania Press.

Ungerson, C. (ed.) (1985) *Women and Social Policy: A Reader*. London: Macmillan.

Walrond-Skinner, S. (ed.) (1981) *Developments in Family Therapy*. London: RKP.

Watson, D. (ed.) (1985) *A Code of Ethics for Social Work: The Second Step*. London: Routledge and Kegan Paul.

Woodhouse, D. and Pengelly, P. (1991) *Anxiety and the Dynamics of Collaboration*. Aberdeen: Aberdeen University Press.

Woodmansey, C. (1985) The post-Seebohm depression, *Journal of Social Work Practice*, 1(4): 3–12.

Woodroofe, K. (1962) *From Charity to Social Work in England and the United States*. London: Routledge and Kegan Paul.

Woolfe, R., Dryden, W. and Charles-Edwards, D. (1989) The nature and range of counselling practice, in W. Dryden, D. Charles-Edwards and R. Woolfe (eds), *Handbook of Counselling in Britain*. London: Routledge.

Worden, W. (1991). *Grief Counselling and Grief Therapy*, 2nd edn. London: Tavistock/Routledge.

Yelloly, M.A. (1980) *Social Work Theory and Psychoanalysis*. London: Van Nostrand Reinhold.

Young, A.F. and Ashton, E.T. (1956) *British Social Work in the Nineteenth Century*. London: Routledge and Kegan Paul.

Young, P. (1967) *The Student and Supervision in Social Work*. London: Routledge and Kegan Paul.

Younghusband, E. (1959) *Report of the Working Party on Social Workers in the Local Authority Health and Welfare Services*. London: HMSO.

Younghusband, E. (1964) *Social Work and Social Change*. London: George Allen and Unwin.

Younghusband, E. (1978) *Social Work in Britain: 1950–1975*. London: George Allen and Unwin.

Index